HAMILTON EAST PUBLIC LIBRARY

P9-CDW-966

393 7

j 915.173 Pan 2010
Pang, Guek-Cheng, 1950-
 Mongolia
 2009022643
 9780761448495

3/10

CULTURES OF THE WORLD
Mongolia

Pang Guek Cheng

Marshall Cavendish
Benchmark
New York

HEPL
1 LIBRARY PLAZA
NOBLESVILLE, IN
46060

PICTURE CREDITS
Cover: © Gavriel Jecan/The Image Bank/Getty Images
alt.type/Reuters: 33, 35, 36, 37 (both), 116, 117 • Bes Stock: 18, 22, 26, 42, 54, 57, 59, 61, 89, 90, 96, 107, 115, 118, 121, 124, 125, 126, 127, 128, 130 • Corbis Inc.: 8, 15, 16, 28, 38, 39, 45, 50, 53, 56, 70, 75, 77, 85, 93, 95, 98, 101, 102, 103, 106, 108, 109 • Getty Images: 43, 47, 78, 79, 110, 119, 129 • Hutchison Library • 71, 104 • Lonely Planet Images: 29, 67, 88 • North Wind Picture Archives: 19, 46 • Photolibrary: 1, 3, 5, 6, 7, 9, 10, 11, 12, 13, 14, 17, 20, 21, 23, 24, 25, 27, 30, 41, 44, 49, 51, 52, 55, 58, 60, 62, 63, 64, 65, 66, 68, 69, 72, 73, 74, 80, 81, 82, 83, 86, 87, 91, 111, 112, 120, 122, 123, 131 • Trip Photographic Library: 76, 94, 97, 99, 100, 105, 113

PRECEDING PAGE
Gorgeous blue mountains and lush green pastures of the Batkhan Reserve in Mongolia.

Publisher (U.S.): Michelle Bisson
Editors: Deborah Grahame, Mindy Pang
Copyreader: Daphne Hougham
Designers: Nancy Sabato, Benson Tan
Cover picture researcher: Connie Gardner
Picture researcher: Thomas Khoo

Marshall Cavendish Benchmark
99 White Plains Road
Tarrytown, NY 10591
Website: www.marshallcavendish.us

© Times Media Private Limited 1999
© Marshall Cavendish International (Asia) Private Limited 2010
® "Cultures of the World" is a registered trademark of Times Publishing Limited.

Originated and designed by Times Media Private Limited
An imprint of Marshall Cavendish International (Asia) Private Limited
A member of Times Publishing Limited

Marshall Cavendish is a trademark of Times Publishing Limited.

All rights reserved. No part of this book may be reproduced or utilized in any form or by any means electronic or mechanical, including photocopying, recording, or by an information storage retrieval system, without permission from the copyright owner.

All Internet sites were correct and accurate at the time of printing. All monetary figures in this publication are in U.S. dollars.

Library of Congress Cataloging-in-Publication Data
Pang, Guek Cheng, 1950-
  Mongolia / Pang Guek Cheng.
     p. cm. — (Cultures of the world)
  Includes bibliographical references and index.
  Summary: "Provides comprehensive information on the geography, history,
    wildlife, governmental structure, economy, cultural diversity, peoples,
    religion, and culture of Mongolia"—Provided by publisher.
  ISBN 978-0-7614-4849-5
  1. Mongolia—Juvenile literature. I. Title.
  DS798.P34 2010
  951.73—dc22   2009022643

Printed in China
7 6 5 4 3 2 1

CONTENTS

INTRODUCTION

WHEN WE THINK OF THE MONGOLS, the picture that comes to mind is that of the fierce and ruthless warriors who swept through Central Asia in the 13th century, cutting a bloody swath across the land and creating the Mongol Empire. We think of Marco Polo, the 13th-century Venetian traveler who ventured east to China and brought back incredible tales of Kublai Khan's court. We see a nomadic people leading a relatively simple life—riding horses, tending their animals, living in tents. More recently, we think also of an undeveloped nation of people who subsisted under communist rule, cut off from the modern world.

Mongolia has been all these things. But today Mongolia is a land of hardy people rich in culture, proud of their history, striving to overcome the strictures of more than six decades of communism. Mongolians are a people in transition, rediscovering their heroes and traditions. They are finding a place for themselves in today's fast-changing world.

GEOGRAPHY

A herd of horses in the Orkhon Valley of the Ovorkhangai *aimag*, or province.

I F YOU LOOK AT A MAP OF ASIA, you will find Mongolia in Northern Asia between two big and powerful countries, Russia and the People's Republic of China. Mongolia is shaped like a pair of smiling lips.

To the north Mongolia shares a border of more than 2,904 miles (4,673 kilometers) with the Siberian part of Russia. In the south Mongolia shares a 3,000-mile (4,830-km) border with China. To the east of Mongolia lies Manchuria and to the west, the Xinjiang Uighur Autonomous Region of the People's Republic of China.

Mountains, plains, and a river in the Ovorkhangai province in Mongolia.

The Mongolian forestry management program ensures that logging does not worsen soil erosion and that reforestation is carried out by replanting trees.

The fertile green Hangai mountain range in Mongolia.

Mongolia is an independent country, not to be confused with Inner Mongolia in north China. The people of the two regions, however, share a similar culture.

Mongolia is slightly smaller than Alaska, with an area of 604,000 square miles (1,564,000 square km). The population is just over 3 million, so there are fewer than three people per square mile (about one person per square km).

HIGH, DRY, AND COLD

Mongolia has a high average altitude of 5,184 feet (1,580 meters), though mountainous areas higher than 12,000 feet (3,658 m) form less than 5 percent of the total land area. About 40 percent of the country lies between 3,000 feet (914 m) and 10,000 feet (3,048 m) above sea level. Even the lowest part, the Höh Nuur depression in the east, is 1,699 feet (518 m) above sea level. The higher areas are in western, northern, and central Mongolia, and the lower elevations are in the east and south.

There are three major mountain ranges in Mongolia—the Altai, the Hangai, and the Hentii. The Altai range in the west and southwest is the largest and highest range in the country. The highest point is the Hüyten peak (Nayramädlïn), which rises to 14,347 feet (4,373 m) above sea level, in the Tavan Bogd Uul mountain group of the Altai range. Much of this range is snow-covered all year round.

The predominantly forested Hangai and Hentii ranges are located in the north-central and northwestern parts of Mongolia. The mountain slopes of these ranges are wooded with cedar, larch, birch, pine, and fir. Above the timberline are alpine meadows with mosses and lichens that bloom in the spring. On the northern part of the Hangai Mountains are a number of extinct volcanoes and volcanic crater lakes. Wild sheep, ibex, and gazelles roam the mountains. The endangered snow leopard inhabits the high mountains along the border with Russia.

Mountaineers from all over the world visit Mongolia to climb the mountains, especially the Altai range. The short mountain-climbing season begins in early July and ends in August.

Winter is bleak at the Altai Mountains in western Mongolia.

THE GOBI DESERT

As part of the government's efforts to conserve the environment, over 13 percent of Mongolian land has been set aside as protected areas. The largest is the Great Gobi Reserve.

In the south-central area lies the famous Gobi Desert, which Mongolia shares with China. The largest desert in Asia, it is also known as Shamo, which means sand in Chinese. The Gobi is the world's coldest, northernmost desert, covering more than 500,000 square miles (1,295,000 square km). Windswept and nearly treeless, surprisingly, only 5 percent of it is sand dunes, while the rest is mostly dry, rocky, and sandy soil. The Gobi is actually a plateau of rolling gravel plains with occasional low ranges and isolated hills. It rises from 3,000 feet (914 m) in the east to 5,000 feet (1,524 m) in the west, where it meets the Altai Mountains. The desert vegetation is grass and scrub. People and livestock there rely on water from small, shallow lakes and wells.

Caravan routes have crisscrossed the Gobi since ancient times. Marco Polo, with his father and his uncle, were the first Europeans to cross the desert, around A.D. 1275. The Gobi is a famous repository of fossils, especially specimens from the Late Cretaceous period—100 million years ago.

A camel caravan at the Khongoryn Els Dune in the Gobi Desert.

DINOSAUR LAND

The naturalist, adventurer, and fossil hunter Roy Chapman Andrews (1884—1960) drove across the Gobi Desert in 1918 and was convinced he had found the Garden of Eden. Andrews worked at the American Museum of Natural History in New York City. He was director of the museum from 1935 to 1942. In 1922, 1923, and 1925, he returned to the Gobi with the museum's first scientific expedition, hoping to find the bones of early humans to confirm the theory that Homo sapiens had evolved in high, dry climates such as those of Central Asia. Instead, he found that the Gobi was a vast repository of dinosaur remains. Andrews discovered the first dinosaur eggs at a time when scientists were not even sure that dinosaurs laid eggs. In On the Trail of Ancient Man, Andrews wrote, "We realized we were looking at the first dinosaur eggs ever seen by a human being. . . . The elongated shape of the eggs was distinctly reptilian." The eggs (like those of the protoceratops fossil) were found in the area of the Gobi called Ulan Usu, which Andrews called the "Flaming Red Cliffs" because its cliffs, buttes, and gullies are made of red rock.

Other expeditions have discovered fossilized animals and plants from the early Paleozoic and Mesozoic eras when this area was covered by great seas and lakes. The Gobi has yielded the skeletons of previously unknown dinosaurs, as well as tiny skulls of some of the earliest identified mammals. The desert fossil beds are extensive and extremely well preserved because of the dry desert climate.

In the 1960s a Mongolian-Polish scientific team discovered skeletons of a velociraptor and a protoceratops that were killed by a violent sandstorm that swept over them as they were trying to kill each other. In 1993 a team from the American Museum of Natural History and the Mongolian Academy of Sciences discovered an oviraptor fossil seated on a clutch of eggs—the first evidence of a dinosaur's showing parental care. Dinosaur exhibits can be seen in the Ulaanbaatar Museum of Natural History.

THE STEPPES

The steppes, or grasslands, mainly cover the eastern part of the country. The vegetation here is made up of varieties of feather grass that are common to the steppes of Central Asia. These grasses sustain the millions of sheep, horses, goats, cattle, and other livestock that graze there. Herds of antelope also roam the grasslands. Livestock are the mainstay of the Mongolian economy.

In the springtime the harsh look that the countryside wears through most of the year changes. It begins to turn a vivid green as everything comes alive, and some hills are carpeted in a tapestry of bright yellow, purple, pale violet, and crimson. Millions of wildflowers burst into bloom to make the most of their short growing season.

Livestock pasturing in the wonderful Mongolian grasslands–the steppes.

Serenity surrounds deep, still Hövsgöl Lake.

RIVERS AND LAKES

Mongolia is a dry land. Total rainfall during the year is only 4 inches (10 centimeters) in the desert and 14 inches (36 cm) in the north. Thus the many rivers, lakes, and glaciers are important sources of water.

Over 1,200 rivers flow in three distinct directions—north into the Arctic Ocean, east into the Pacific Ocean, and south into the desert. The longest rivers are the Selenge, one of the rivers flowing into Lake Baikal in Russia; the Orhon, a tributary of the Selenge; and the Tuul. The source of all three is in the Hangai range. The Herlen and Orhon rivers originate in the Hentii range. A vital resource of water for years to come, there are about 200 glaciers in the Altai Mountains alone.

Mongolia has more than 4,000 lakes. Many are small, with an average surface area of 2 square miles (5 square km), but the total area of all the lakes is just over 1 percent of Mongolia's land area. Many lakes were formed by glacial and volcanic activity and are concentrated between the Altai and the Hangai ranges. The Har Us is a saltwater lake and the largest in Mongolia. The Hövsgöl is the deepest lake in both Mongolia and all of Central Asia.

Mongolians are being taught that with limited water resources the rivers and lakes must be protected and the dumping of garbage and sewage must be stopped.

LONG, COLD WINTERS

"The real summer lasts only from May till August. Then, the valleys are like an exquisite garden and the woods are ablaze with color. Bluebells, their stalks bending under the weight of blossoms, clothe every hillside in a glorious azure dress bespangled with yellow roses, daisies, and forget-me-nots."
–Roy Chapman Andrews in *Across Mongolian Plains*

Mongolia lies between latitude 46°N and longitude 105°E, in the same belt as Ukraine, Romania, Hungary, Austria, and northern United States. The country is totally landlocked; the nearest sea is the Yellow Sea, about 435 miles (700 km) beyond the eastern border.

Mongolia has a continental climate characterized by extreme temperature changes. From November to March average temperatures are below freezing. The coldest month is usually January, when temperatures can drop to as low as -9°F (-23°C).

In the summer, the hottest month is usually July, when temperatures range from 68°F (20°C) in the northern regions to about 50°F—80°F (10°C—27°C) in the south. Temperature changes of as many degrees as 35°F—55°F (2°C—13°C) can occur in one day.

The sparkling white snow of Mongolia is beautiful but extremely harsh and cold for living.

THE IMMORTAL BLUE SKY

The distance from the sea and the fact that any moisture-laden winds from the east encounter a mountain range ensure that the winds that blow over Mongolia are dry. Mongolia has very little rainfall, although the mountainous regions of the north are wetter than the southern parts. The rainy season is between May and September.

The lack of humidity means that on most days the sun shines brightly from a blue and often cloudless sky. Mongolians boast that they can bask in as many as 250 sunny days a year. Traditional Mongolians believe the immense blue sky is the Supreme God called Tengri (TENG-ri). For Mongolians, blue is a lucky color, and is incorporated in their national emblem.

Mongolia is also known as the land of winds because of the sharp gusts that blow in the springtime and often become storms.

DISTINCTIVE FAUNA

The Asian, or Bactrian, camels of Mongolia are among the remaining 700,000 Asian camels in the world. These camels have two humps and are smaller than the Arabian camel, or dromedary. They graze on the sparse desert grasses and can live for three months on water alone.

Rainbows over the cloudless blue skies of Hövsgöl Lake.

The Mongolian horse is small, has a thick, well-muscled neck, and a very bulky head. It is remarkably tough and can easily survive harsh winters. It resembles the Przewalski's horse, a rare species of wild horse that once roamed the Gobi Desert and the steppes in great numbers and that has narrowly avoided extinction. Unlike the more common domesticated breeds, Przewalski's are nearly impossible to tame.

Mongolia is a resting point for migratory birds that fly from the northern parts of the Asian continent to the warmer shores of the Indian and Pacific oceans in the winter. These are mainly waterfowl and other birds that live near water.

A range of concrete houses and nomadic yurts dots the aerial landscape of the capital city of Mongolia, Ulaanbaatar.

SMALL-TOWN MONGOLIA

Most Mongolians live in the countryside in small towns. The facilities in such towns usually include concrete municipal office buildings, a central square, a dilapidated power station, and a reserve fuel dump on the outskirts to supply the trucks passing by. Residents live in concrete apartment buildings or in *gers*, also called yurts—traditional structures made of a wooden frame covered with layers of felt. A wooden fence surrounds each *ger* so that it can be assigned a house number. The town administration provides the residents with postal and other services. Sometimes there are also communities of several hundred *gers* laid out in blocks separated by roads.

The capital city, Ulaanbaatar, earlier known as Urga, was founded in 1639. Its name changed many times before becoming Ulaanbaatar ("Red Hero") in 1924. The settlement was once a center of Buddhism and the residence of the Bogdo Khan, a religious leader. The city of some 994,300 (2006 estimate) lies in the Tuul River valley of north-central Mongolia. It is the political, cultural, economic, and industrial center of the country and the only big city in terms of population. About a third of the entire Mongolian population lives in modern Ulaanbaatar.

Darkhan, north of the capital, is the second-largest city, with about 87,800 residents. It is an industrial center built from the ground up in 1961 in an area rich in limestone, sand, clay, marble, and coal—materials important in construction. Darkhan is the hub of the construction industry and also produces consumer goods and foodstuffs.

Erdenet has the third-largest population, around 79,647, and lies in the north, between the Selenge and Orhon rivers. The town grew around an ore-dressing plant that was built in 1973. The plant is the fourth-largest copper plant in the world and produces approximately 130,000 tons (117,910 metric tons) of copper concentrate annually.

Ulaanbaatar, the capital city of Mongolia, is connected to both the Chinese railway system and the Russian Trans-Siberian Railroad.

HISTORY

This Genghis Khan statue sits before the Parliament
Palace on Sukhbaatar Square in Ulaanbaatar.

THE AGGRESSIVE MONGOLS RODE out of the heart of Asia in the 13th century and subjugated all the nations from Central Asia to the banks of the Danube River. China remained under Mongolian domination for more than a century, Russia for more than two centuries.

NOMADIC TRIBES

The steppes of Central Asia were inhabited by nomadic tribes, probably of Turkic, Tataric, or Ugrian origin, before the Mongolian nation emerged. The Chinese emperor Shi Huang Di built the first part of the Great Wall

Early nomadic tribes using wagons to move their yurts, or *gers*, circular felt dwellings.

As the young Temüjin began to gather followers and grow in power, one of the tribes he defeated and mercilessly exterminated were the Tatars who had killed his father. The Europeans confused the name Tatars with the similar-sounding Tartarus, a region of hell in Greek mythology. They called the Mongols by that name because their behavior was seen as hellish.

of China to keep out these marauding tribes, specifically the Xiongnu, believed to be related to the Huns, another fierce band of conquerors. The famous tomb that contains over 6,000 life-size terra-cotta figures of soldiers and horses is that of Shi Huang Di .

In 209 B.C., the Huns established the first state in Central Asia. The Huns later split into two groups. One went west, moving from the steppes north of the Caspian Sea to the Roman Empire during the fourth and fifth centuries. The other group entered the Han and Xia lands south of the Great Wall.

From the 7th to the 10th century, nomadic peoples, including the Avars, Turks, Uighur, and Kitan, successively rose to power, became fragmented, and moved westward, or came to be integrated with the Chinese.

The Mongols were a small group of such nomadic people who moved from pasture to pasture with the seasons. They fought with each other and formed alliances when defeated in battle or when it was in their best interests to do so. These alliances would change according to the shifting strengths of the different clans.

The rise of the Mongol people began in the time of Chinggis Khan (1167—1227), commonly

The legendary Genghis Khan, Mongol warrior and conqueror.

known as Genghis Khan. He was the first ruler of Mongolia to unite the tribes of Central Asia. Before he became ruler, his name was Temüjin. He inherited the leadership of his clan from his father and gained greater power by conquering or forging alliances with the other clans.

In 1206, at a great assembly of all the tribes, Temüjin was proclaimed Genghis Khan, meaning "strong ruler," and all the clans agreed to adopt the name Mongol.

Unlike the European knight of antiquity, the Mongol cavalryman was lightly armored. He was clad in leather armor, which gave him greater agility than metal armor would have. He carried a small leather shield on his left arm for protection. His weapons included a lance, a bow with a quiver of arrows, a saber, and a dagger. He had arrows for different purposes, some with heads designed solely for killing that whistled when released to terrify the enemy, and others that whistled but only wounded the enemy. The Mongol bowman was trained to shoot while riding at full gallop and was equally adept at hitting targets in front of him as well as behind him.

A herd of fresh horses was always kept ready, and each cavalryman had a reserve of up to four remounts. As part of their basic training, soldiers joined an annual game hunt in which wild animals were chased into a given area and shot by horsemen. Each soldier was given just one arrow to kill the animal of his choice.

Artillerymen with mangonels, or giant catapults, supported the cavalry. When laying siege to a town, Mongols used these to hurl stones, rocks, trees, and even animal corpses to breach the walls.

THE MONGOL EMPIRE

Genghis began building his empire in 1209 with a campaign against the southern kingdom of Xi Xia, ruled by the Tanguts, who controlled the vital oases along the Silk Road linking China with Rome. Caravans, including those of the Mongols, traveled the route carrying all kinds of goods and were heavily taxed by the Tanguts. Defeated in 1210, Xi Xia became Mongolia's first vassal state.

The yellow area in this map represents the Mongol Empire at the height of its expansion from the blue area it was before.

Next to be conquered was the Jin Empire, which was already struggling with internal troubles. Other conquests soon followed. The Mongols expanded west, defeating the Kara-Khitai Empire west of the Altai Mountains and the cities of Samarkand, Bukhara, Merv, and Herat, belonging to the Muslim empire of Khwarizm. The Mongols forged into Russian territory and threatened to conquer the Russian principalities of Kiev, Chernigov, Galicia, Rostov, and Suzdal, before deciding to return to their homeland in Central Asia.

Many clans caught in the Mongol onslaught chose to submit rather than be killed. They paid taxes and provided men to the army, adding to Mongol military strength. Chinese, Turks, Persians, Armenians, Georgians, and others fought alongside Mongol soldiers. Skilled craftsmen, musicians, scholars, and administrators were taken prisoner to serve the khan. Millions of people were subjugated. The wars of this period caused great destruction. These wars unified Asian and European tribes, however, and for a very long time brought Eastern and Western civilizations face-to-face.

Genghis Khan died in 1227 of a fall from a horse at the age of 60. By 1280 the Mongol Empire built by Genghis, his sons Jochi, Chaghatai, Ogodei, and Tolui, and his grandsons stretched over all of Asia almost to the Mediterranean Sea. But the empire soon began to break down into smaller, independent fiefdoms ruled by different branches of the family.

SONS OF GENGHIS

After Genghis died, his son Ogodei was chosen in 1229 to be the Great Khan. Ogodei continued to expand the empire. He subdued Xi Xia, which had rebelled, continued the efforts to annex the rich Song Empire, and sent a new army to the west.

He made Karakorum his capital, transforming it from a simple base camp into a great walled city with the labor of captive skilled craftsmen. News of its splendors spread to the West. In 1238 the Mongols under Batu, Jochi's son, attacked and defeated Russia, a few principalities at a time, and moved on to Poland and Hungary in 1241. The Mongols then rode into Austria. When they had almost reached Vienna, news of Ogodei's death in 1241 arrived from Karakorum, and they withdrew.

In the following years, there was a prolonged power struggle between Batu and his cousin Guyuk, Ogodei's son. Batu remained in southern Russia, where he established his own capital, Sarai, and ruled his fiefdom, known as the Golden Horde. Power then passed to the sons of Tolui.

Mongke, Tolui's eldest son, was enthroned in 1251, and with his brother Kublai renewed the assault against the Song. Another brother, Hulagu, attacked Baghdad, the heart of the Muslim world. The caliph (ruler) and his family were massacred, and the Muslim empire became an Ilkhanate (subordinate khanate), ruled by Hulagu. His lands stretched from present-day Pakistan to Turkey. After Mongke died in 1259, a power struggle ensued between Kublai, still battling the Song, and Arigh Boke, the youngest brother, in Karakorum. Kublai returned to Mongolia and fought Arigh Boke, winning power in 1264. He proclaimed himself Great Khan. By this time the powerful Mongol Empire had broken into fiefdoms.

Kublai spent much time in northern China (modern Inner Mongolia) and established a capital at Shangdu. He set himself the task of developing and unifying China. He founded the Yuan dynasty and moved his capital to the more centrally located Dadu (present-day Beijing). He encouraged trade, improved Chinese agriculture, advanced the study of the sciences, and developed a written script for the Mongolian language. In 1279 he finally

On his deathbed, Genghis Khan urges his sons to unite by demonstrating how a single arrow can be easily broken, but it is almost impossible to break four arrows together.

An engraving of Kublai Khan.

The fall of the Mongols coincided with the advance of the Manchu cannons and muskets, which the Mongols could not match. The Mongols were pushed by the Manchus from the north and the west, and by the Russians from the south and the east.

defeated the Song Empire and united north and south China. He attempted to invade Japan in 1274 and 1281, and Java in Southeast Asia in 1292, but without success. Kublai Khan died in 1294 at the age of 79.

The Mongols' 89-year rule of China, as the Yuan dynasty, ended in 1368, when the Chinese rebelled—tired of the ever-increasing taxes and the corruption of the officials. The Mongols were forced back to Mongolia by the succeeding Ming dynasty, whose rulers rebuilt the Great Wall of China to ensure that the Mongols and other marauding tribes were kept out for good.

THE DECLINE OF THE MONGOLS

After their defeat in China, the Mongols retreated to their homeland. Over the next few centuries the unity that had bound together their great empire dissolved as the various clans jostled for power. Moreover, the Mongols were being squeezed between Russia and China. The Manchus—inhabitants of Manchuria—of northeast China had assumed power in China and formed the Qing dynasty (1644–1911). Russia and China had been making alliances, meanwhile, and rapidly expanding their influence in the area. From the 14th century until Mongolia became a people's republic in the early 20th century, events in both Russia and China had a significant impact on Mongolia.

From the 14th to the 17th centuries, the Mongol tribes fought among themselves. The Oirads in the west split with the Khalkhas in the east. Eventually these two remaining big groups splintered into smaller tribes that continued bickering among themselves, thus allowing the Chinese to invade and control them. The various fragmented tribes became the vassals of China.

In the late 16th century Buddhism took hold in Mongolia. Gombordorji Zanabazar (1635–1723), the six-year-old young son of a wealthy prince, was proclaimed leader of the Buddhists in 1641; he was called the Jebtsundamba Khutuktu, which means "reincarnate lama."

During the 1750s the Manchus decided, for administrative purposes, to divide Mongolia into northern and southern regions. Known as Inner Mongolia, the southern provinces were essentially part of China. The northern provinces were called Outer Mongolia.

Chinese traders and moneylenders played a defining role in Mongolian society. The Mongolians fell increasingly into debt to the Manchus, were forced to pay high taxes, and were resentful of being dominated by them. So when the Manchus were overthrown in 1911, the time the Republic of China was formed, it was an opportunity for Outer Mongolia, with Russia's support, to declare its independence.

The Winter Palace of Bodgo Khan is now a museum.

GOD-KING AND DIVINE PLANS

The Mongolian revolt was led by the eighth Jebtsundamba Khutuktu who ruled Mongolia with the consent of the Manchus. He was called the Bogdo Khan, champion of God and supporter of civilization, and revered as a god-king, uniting state and religion. He backed Mongolian nationalistic ambitions with the aim of reuniting Mongolia once more. He even tried to reclaim the territory of Inner Mongolia from China. The god-king was also a drunkard and a womanizer who supported his decadent lifestyle by selling his blessings to the people.

In 1915, with Russian support, Mongolia was able to persuade China to sign a treaty involving all three countries. According to this treaty, the Chinese were forced to recognize Outer Mongolia's independence while retaining control of Inner Mongolia. But in 1919 Chinese troops invaded Mongolia and imprisoned the Bogdo Khan. Russia, caught up in the upheaval of the Russian Revolution and World War I, was unable to help.

A statue of Vladimir Lenin, the Russian revolutionist, in Ulaanbaatar.

Deliverance from the Chinese this time came through a strange and colorful figure, Baron Roman Feodorovich von Ungern-Sternberg, also known as the Mad Baron. He was a Russian czarist general who had escaped the revolution in Russia. He believed he was part of a divine plan to liberate Mongolia. In 1921, with an army of opportunists, including Russians, Mongolians, Tibetans, and Poles, the baron attacked Urga, drove out the Chinese army, and rescued the Bogdo Khan.

Having helped Mongolia, the Mad Baron felt that the divine plan also called for him to save Russia from the communists—giving Russia an excuse to intervene in Mongolian affairs.

A REVOLUTION TAKES PLACE

Meanwhile, nationalistic feelings were on the rise in Mongolia. The people were increasingly opposed to the Chinese invaders as well as to the Mad Baron and his White Russian army, which was turning out to be an army of occupation. When the Chinese invaded Mongolia in 1919, a group of Mongolian nationalists fled across the border to Siberia and formed the Mongolian People's Revolutionary Party (MPRP). Among them were the revolutionary leaders Damdin Sukhbaatar and Horlyn Choibalsan.

When the Mad Baron drove out the Chinese occupiers in February 1921 and declared an independent Mongolia, the revolutionaries' task became twice as difficult. Mongolia had to be freed first from the Chinese and then from the White Russian army. But in March 1921, with the backing of socialist Russia, which in 1917 had undergone a revolution bringing down the czar, Sukhbaatar crossed the border and drove out both the Chinese and the White Russians and pushed on to capture Urga.

Independence was declared on July 11, 1921. The Bogdo Khan was allowed to remain as head of state, making Mongolia a republican monarchy from 1921 to 1924. When he died in 1924, there was no attempt to find a successor.

DAMDIN SUKHBAATAR

Damdin Sukhbaatar (1893—1923)—sukhbaatar means "ax hero"—was conscripted into the Mongolian army when he was 19. As he was very intelligent and a natural leader, he soon became a junior noncommissioned officer (NCO). After distinguishing himself in border clashes with the Chinese, he was promoted to senior NCO.

When the Chinese invaded Mongolia in 1919, he joined a small group of like-minded army friends to plan a revolution. With the help of Russian agents, Sukhbaatar's group and a similar nationalist group led by Horlyn Choibalsan fled to Siberia, where they received military training from the Russians. When Baron Roman Feodorovich von Ungern-Sternberg drove out the Chinese, Sukhbaatar and his followers moved to Hiagt (now Troitskosavsk) on the Russian border and formed the Mongolian People's Revolutionary Party.

In March 1921 Sukhbaatar crossed the border and drove the Chinese out of the town of Amgalanbaatar. He made it a provisional capital, renaming it Altanbulag.

The baron attacked the revolutionary government. Sukhbaatar, Choibalsan, and the Russian army repulsed his attack, captured the capital city of Urga, and proclaimed the independence of Mongolia on July 11, 1921.

Sukhbaatar died mysteriously in 1923 at the age of 30. His body is buried in a cemetery outside Ulaanbaatar. A statue of the young nationalist astride a horse stands there in his honor. He is regarded as Mongolia's greatest revolutionary hero.

The base of the statue of Damdin Sukhbaatar in Ulaanbaatar is engraved with words attributed to him: "If we, all the people, are united in common effort and common will, there can be nothing in the world that we cannot achieve, that we will not have learned, or failed to do."

In 1924 Mongolia was declared the Mongolian People's Republic. The country once again was closed to the outside world. Joseph Stalin's policies in the Soviet Union had far-reaching effects on Mongolia; there were campaigns of political terror, purges, arrests, and an attack against the Mongolian feudal culture. In 1929, when Stalin launched the policy of collectivization, Mongolia was expected to do the same. Hundreds of Russian advisers and technicians were brought in to help. This communist, Soviet-style republic with a one-party system remained in power until 1990.

A painting of Vladimir Lenin, Russian communist leader, and Mongolian revolutionary head Horlyn Choibalsan.

The Russian Revolution of October 1917 was the Bolshevik party's forces fighting successfully against the White Russian army of the czar. The Bolsheviks, who became the communists, also helped the Mongolian nationalists in their own struggle for independence.

COMMUNIST MONGOLIA

Stalin's puppet in Mongolia was Marshal Horlyn Choibalsan; he was one of the founders of the Mongolian People's Revolutionary Party and controlled the government, army, and secret police. Mongolian livestock herders were divided into rich and poor. Anyone with more than 200 sheep was considered rich, and his animals were seized and given to the poor. Property was appropriated from the Buddhist monasteries; thousands of lamas were killed outright, and hundreds of temples and monasteries were destroyed. Chinese businessmen and their families were expelled from the country.

In 1931 Japan invaded Manchuria and threatened to overrun Mongolia, but joint Soviet-Mongolian forces met that threat successfully. Subsequently, Russia and China signed an anti-Japanese treaty that also recognized Mongolia's independence.

When Choibalsan died in 1952, Yumjaagiyn Tsedenbal became president. During his long tenure (1952—84), he promoted Russian culture. Everyone had to speak Russian, schools and universities taught in Russian, and people wore Western-style clothing instead of the *del*, the traditional Mongolian dress. Intellectuals were persecuted for expressing independent views. Tsedenbal was ousted in 1984.

DEMOCRATIC CHANGES

In the late 1980s the Soviet Union implemented perestroika and glasnost, surprisingly liberal policies calling for restructuring the economy and greater openness in political affairs. Jambyn Batmönh, who succeeded Tsedenbal, reorganized the government and decentralized the economy. In July 1990 the first free elections were held. Since the move to democracy, the Mongolian government has generally been formed by the former communist party, the Mongolian People's Revolutionary Party (MPRP). The sole exception was the administration of the Democratic Party from 1996 until 2000. Since 2004, the MPRP has run the country in coalition with a number of smaller parties.

The transition to democracy and a free-market system has not been without its growing pains. Over the last decade a number of demonstrations have taken place pushing for legal reform, mostly in the area of land management and ownership. These protests have generally been peaceful and have actually helped enable the privatization of land. Sadly, not all demonstrations have gone so smoothly. In 2008 hundreds of demonstrators took to the streets of Ulaanbaatar and set fire to the MPRP headquarters to protest alleged election fraud by the MPRP. While these claims were largely discounted, the riot resulted in five deaths, hundreds of injuries, and the imposition of a four-day state of emergency.

The Russian Communist Zaisan Memorial in Ulaanbaatar honors Soviet and Mongolian soldiers of World War II.

GOVERNMENT

The Parliament Palace and government house at Sukhbaatar Square in Ulaanbaatar.

MONGOLIA IS IN A STATE OF transition. It was a feudal society for much of its premodern history, entered the 20th century as a socialist state, and moved into the 21st century in search of democracy. For more than 65 years of its recent political history, Mongolia was a communist state under the influence of the Soviet Union, cut off from the rest of the world.

When the dismantling of communism took place in the Soviet Union and other East European countries, and when student protests occurred in China, Mongolians also demonstrated for change. Today Mongolia embraces a democratic system of government and is learning to take its place in the world of nations.

REINS OF POWER

Mongolia has a parliamentary government. The State Great Hural (HOO-rahl), or parliament, is the highest legislative body in the land. The State Great Hural, a unicameral assembly, has 76 members. It appoints the prime minister and members of his cabinet, which is the highest executive body of the state and ensures that all policies of the State Great Hural are implemented. It also oversees the activities of the smaller local governments. The national government is led by a president, elected by popular vote. Though the president has powers of veto and has other responsibilities, he is primarily a symbolic figure.

After Mongolia declared independence in 1921, the first noncommunist country to give it recognition was India, in 1955. Mongolia became a member of the United Nations in 1961 and was given diplomatic recognition by the United Kingdom and other West European and developing countries in 1963. The United States recognized Mongolia in 1987.

The Supreme Court, which includes the chief justice and other judges, is the highest judicial authority in the land. Judges are elected by the State Great Hural for four-year terms.

The Mongolian legal system is a blend of Russian, Chinese, and Turkish law. Civil law, which is closely modeled on the Russian system, governs relations between people, protecting their rights and the rights of the family. Civil and criminal cases are settled in the people's district courts and provincial courts.

LOCAL ADMINISTRATION

In order to govern Mongolia's large area, the country is divided into 22 administrative regions: 21 *aimags* (or *aymags*, AI-mugs), or provinces, and the municipality of Ulaanbaatar. The largest *aimag* is the Gobi Desert region of Umnugov. That area has 63,690 square miles (165,000 square km) of land, a very rigorous climate, and is the most sparsely populated *aimag*, with only 49,600 people.

Each *aimag* is divided into smaller districts, of which there are 315 in Mongolia. The *aimags* are governed by small legislative councils called *hural*. Deputies, or representatives of the people, are elected to the *hural* for four-year terms.

POLITICAL UPHEAVAL

Toward the end of the 1980s, the changes in European communist countries began to have similar impacts on Mongolia. Several newly formed opposition parties organized peaceful demonstrations, demanding political and economic reforms. The most prominent of these fledgling parties was the Mongolian Democratic Union, founded in December 1989.

Opposite:
Musical performances are often held during the MPRP election campaign rallies.

As new opposition groups emerged and public rallies increased, a crisis of confidence occurred within the ruling Mongolian People's Revolutionary Party (MPRP), and the entire communist leadership of Mongolia resigned. The prime minister, Jambyn Batmönh, was replaced by Punsalmaagiyn Ochirbat as head of government in 1990.

THE MONGOLIAN PEOPLE'S REVOLUTIONARY PARTY

The Mongolian People's Revolutionary Party (MPRP) is Mongolia's oldest—and for a very long time the only—political party in the nation. It ruled the country from 1921 until 1996 and again between 2000 and 2004. Before the revolution of 1921, there were no political parties in Mongolia.

The MPRP was established on March 1, 1921, at a meeting of 17 Mongolian revolutionaries in the border town of Hiagt (now Troitskosavsk in Russia). Since 2006 it has been the foremost group in a number of coalition governments. The leader or chairman of the party is the country's current prime minister, Sanjaa Bayar. The general secretary of the party is Khurelsukh Ukhnaa. Since the move toward greater political freedom and expression began in the 1990s, the MPRP has shed its former Marxist-Leninist communist philosophy. Instead, now it proclaims democratic socialist principles. The party has more than 80,000 members.

The ruling party responded to the people's demands, expelling Yumjaagiyn Tsedenbal, its general party secretary, and rehabilitating those purged by him in the 1960s. Foreign investments were encouraged through new laws. Previously, the communist government had enforced collective ownership of all livestock—everything was owned by the state, and the number of animals people could own personally was limited. Such limitations have been removed, and new opposition parties were legalized.

In July 1990 the first democratic general election was held. This brought into existence a parliamentary government with a president and, for the first time, representatives from more than one political party in the State Great Hural.

In the years following the 1992 election, the opposition parties regrouped. Four of them formed the Mongolian National Democratic Party, and another four parties became the Coalition of Four Unions. A United Heritage Party emerged as well as the Mongolian Democratic Renewal Party. All of them pressured the government for change and improvements in the people's living standards. Demonstrations and hunger strikes were held in Sukhbaatar Square from 1993 to 1995.

Still, the MPRP had held on to its strong control over government. Of the 430 deputies in the State Great Hural, 357 were MPRP candidates. Also elected were candidates from the Mongolian Democratic Party, the Mongolian Revolutionary Youth League, the Mongolian National Progress Party, and the Mongolian Social-Democratic Party, as well as some independent candidates.

A new constitution in 1992 made two important changes: it reduced the number of members of the State Great Hural to 76, all belonging to the sole legislative house, and it changed the name of the country from the Mongolian People's Republic to, simply, Mongolia. The election results that year showed that the MPRP was still popular; it won 70 out of the 76 seats.

The 1996 election gave the opposition parties their first victory. The Democratic Alliance, a coalition of several opposition parties, won 50 seats in the State Great Hural. The MPRP took only 25 seats, and the United Heritage Party one.

Radnaasumbereliyn Gonchigdorj, the leader of the Mongolian Social Democratic Party (a member of the Democratic Alliance), became chairman of the State Great Hural. The leader of the Democratic Alliance, Mendsaikhanu Enkhsaikhan, became the prime minister. The president continued to be Punsalmaagiyn Ochirbat, who replaced Jambyn Batmönh in 1990 and had had his position confirmed by the people in direct elections in 1993. By May 1997, however, Ochirbat's popularity had waned. He lost the presidential election that year to Natsagiin Bagabandi, chairman of the MPRP.

On April 23, 1998, Tsakhiagiin Elbegdorj, leader of the Democracy Union coalition, (also known as Elbegdorj Tsahia) became Mongolia's youngest prime minister. During the 2000 elections the Mongolian first-past-the-post electoral system—the persons with the most votes win—enabled the MPRP to win 95 percent of the seats in parliament with only 52 percent of the popular vote. This new government was led by then Prime Minister Nambaryn Enkhbayar. In 2001 the government amended the constitution to limit one of the main presidential powers, that of nominating the prime minister, to his only naming the candidate proposed by the ruling party. The 2004 elections saw a nearly fifty-fifty split between the MPRP and the Democratic Party; the latter formed a new government under Prime Minister Tsakhiagiin Elbegdorj. This government, however, was short-lived. In 2006 the 10 MPRP ministers resigned from the government coalition, leading to the dissolution of the government and the formation of a new coalition government under the MPRP led by Prime Minister Miyeegombo Enkhbold.

In October 2007 the prime minister was ousted by the MPRP and replaced by its new leader Sanjaa Bayar. The parliamentary elections of 2008 gave the MPRP a significant majority but triggered violent protests outside the MPRP headquarters because of allegations of vote rigging and election fraud. At least five people were killed and hundreds injured before a state of emergency was declared. Nevertheless, Nambaryn Enkhbayar retained his presidency until the May 2009 elections, when Tsakhiagiin Elbegdorj began his term.

Mongolian women casting their ballots during the 2009 elections, below a fanciful schoolroom mural.

INDEPENDENT AND SOVEREIGN

The constitution of Mongolia was adopted in 1960. It was changed in 1992 and further revised in 1996 and 2001. In its present form, it has shed much of its former communist ideology and now reflects the move toward democratic reform of the government and an open-market economy.

The constitution proclaims Mongolia to be an independent and sovereign republic. It upholds the ideals of democracy, justice, freedom, equality, national unity, and respect for the law. Total power is vested in the people and is exercised through their direct participation in state affairs and through elected representatives.

The state recognizes all forms of public and private property, including private ownership of land, but reserves the right to confiscate private land if it has been used for a purpose contrary to the national interest.

Basic human rights and freedoms are guaranteed, including social assistance entitlements in old age, disability, childbirth, and child care. All citizens have the right to free medical care and free basic education.

ROLE OF THE ARMY

The Mongolian army was at its most formidable in the 13th to the 16th centuries, at the height of the great Mongol Empire. The modern Mongolian army traces its beginnings to March 1921 when the rebel forces under Damdin Sukhbaatar and Horlyn Choibalsan defeated both Chinese and White Russian army forces to liberate Mongolia from foreign invaders. In 1939 Mongolian forces helped Soviet forces repel a Japanese invasion from Manchuria. Mongolia also gave support to Soviet forces during World War II.

Mongolian soldiers on parade at the opening ceremony of the Naadam festival.

Today the armed forces are made up of troops for general defense, air defense, construction, and civil defense. All Mongolian males above the age of 18 are obliged by law to do active military service for one year. Those who have fulfilled their service are enrolled in the reserves. The Mongolian army has been involved in UN peacekeeping operations in Sierra Leone and Kosovo, and it has also assisted the United States with troop detachments in both Iraq and Afghanistan.

FOREIGN RELATIONS

In the 1990s, despite reforms toward democratic freedoms and a market economy, bonds with the Russian Federation (Russia) and the other newly independent socialist countries continued to be strong. Ties with China improved as well, although historically they have not been smooth. Mongolia maintains good relations with numerous other nations, including the United States, Canada, South Korea, and Japan.

Sanjaa Bayar *(1956—), the current prime minister of Mongolia, was elected on November 22, 2007. Born in Ulaanbaatar, he left to study law at the state university in Moscow. On his return to Mongolia, he served in the General Staff of Mongolia (1979—83) and worked as a journalist and editor for the Montsame and Mongolpress news agencies (1983—90) before entering politics as a member of the State Baga Hural (1990—92). From 1992 until 1997 he was a lecturer at the Academy of State and Society Studies, a researcher at Washington State University, and director of the Institute for Strategic Studies of Mongolia. In 1997 Bayar became the Presidential Chief of Staff, after which, in 2001, he was appointed as Mongolia's ambassador to Russia. He also served as secretary general for the MPRP from 2005 to 2007. In February 2009 he suffered a horse-riding accident, causing serious injuries that left him bedridden for weeks. But the youthful prime minister is able to perform his duties.*

Nambaryn Enkhbayar *(1958—) was born in the Mongolian capital, Ulaanbaatar, where he lived until leaving Mongolia to study at the Moscow Institute of Literature, where he earned an undergraduate degree in literature and language in 1980. In 1985 and 1986 he attended Leeds University in England where he studied English. Between 1980 and 1990 he worked as a translator, editor, secretary general, vice president, and eventually president of the Mongolian Writers' Union. Following the democratization of Mongolia in 1990, he entered politics and served as vice chair of the government arts committee until 1992 when he was elected to a seat in parliament and became the minister of culture for the MPRP government. When the MPRP lost the 1996 elections, Enkhbayar became the head of the opposition. In 2000 he was elected unanimously to the office of prime minister; he later became the speaker of parliament in 2004. He was elected president on June 24, 2005, with over 53 percent of the popular vote, well ahead of his closest rival. His presidenial term ended in May 2009.*

ECONOMY

A gleaming new office building towers over the older residential buildings in Ulaanbaatar.

CHAPTER 4

MONGOLIA'S ECONOMIC development can be divided into three periods: the traditional economy before the revolution, the socialist economy after 1921, and the emerging market economy from the late 1980s to the present. The nation now is transitioning toward an open-market economy.

Earlier, during the socialist period, the government set production quotas for farms and factories. Today its goal is to revive the national economy by increasing the proportion of private ownership and creating favorable conditions for foreign investment. Individual enterprise is encouraged. The nomadic sheep or cattle herder is still important to the economy no less than the urban entrepreneur.

The State Property Committee is responsible for implementing and monitoring the privatization program adopted by the government in July 1997. The committee determines all privatization policies and other procedures.

A truck at the Erdenet Copper Mines. One of the largest mines in the world, the copper ore and other metals there contribute to a share of Mongolia's economy.

THREE ECONOMIC REGIONS

In the late 1980s Mongolia was divided into three economic regions. Today, the central region is the most productive. It covers the Selenge, Bulgan, Hövsgöl, Töv, Arhangai, Övöhangai, Bayanhongor, Dundgov', Önögov', and Dornogov' aimags. About 70 percent of the population lives in this region, which includes the major industrial centers of Ulaanbaatar, Darkhan, and Erdenet. It has the richest mineral deposits, the best agricultural land, and the most developed network of power supply, transportation, and communications. It is responsible for about 90 percent of the national industrial output and more than 60 percent of the national agricultural yield.

The eastern economic region consists of the Sukhbaatar, Dornod, and Hentii aimags. It occupies a quarter of the country, and about a tenth of the people live there. Most of the land is steppeland, which is fertile pastureland. The area is rich in mining, mainly of tungsten, fluorspar, and brown coal. It is also responsible for about 8 percent of the national industrial production and 15 percent of the national agricultural output.

The western economic region includes the Bayan-Ölgi, Uvs, Hovd, Zavhan, and Gov'altai aimags. It is somewhat more populated than the eastern region—more than 20 percent of the population lives there—but it contributes only 5 percent to the national industrial output and about 20 percent to the national agricultural harvest. Nevertheless, the western region is believed to be economically promising, especially in mineral resources, which remain to be developed. Animal herding by-products, timber and other building materials, and minerals make up the region's share of the national commerce.

CHANGE IN THE 20TH CENTURY

Traditionally, Mongolia's subsistence economy (providing just enough for a family's needs) was based on nomadic animal husbandry. Most of the population were herders. Herders owned livestock or tended the herds belonging to the rich or the monasteries. They produced necessities from the animals, kept what they needed, and gave the rest in rent. There was hardly any farming or industry. Trade and businesses were run mostly by the Chinese.

After the revolution in 1921 the communist government began to grow crops and launch industries based on the processing of animal products. Mining, forestry, and consumer goods industries as well as railway and industrial complexes were developed. The government controlled all trade, finance, transportation, and communications. Collectivization was introduced, livestock taken over from private owners, and state farms established. All production targets were set by the state in five-year plans.

In the late 1980s, however, it dawned on the government that there was overcentralization and that production goals were being met regardless of the many costs. So the government introduced democratic reforms. Since its privatization policy was implemented, more than 30,000 private businesses have started up, helped by a significant increase in foreign investment.

ANIMAL HUSBANDRY AND AGRICULTURE

Raising livestock is still the principal economic activity in Mongolia. The main food product of Mongols is meat. Since collectivization was reversed, herders are allowed to own more animals. Limits on private ownership have been removed. By 1999 more than 96 percent of all livestock was privately owned.

A shepherd tending his flock of sheep on the grasslands of Mongolia.

Timber logs being hauled by rail for export.

There are more than 14 million sheep, over 45 percent of all livestock. Wool is produced from sheep and camels. Cattle, horses, goats, and camels provide meat, skins, and milk. Mongolia has industrial cattle farms and mechanized dairies. About 2 million gallons or more (some 7.6 million liters) of *airag* (AI-rug), an alcoholic drink made from mare's milk, are consumed annually.

Farming in Mongolia is very limited and difficult due to the harsh climate. The main crops are grains, mainly wheat. Barley, oats, and millet are grown mostly as fodder for the livestock. Potatoes, cabbages, carrots, turnips, onions, garlic, cucumbers, tomatoes, and lettuce are the main vegetables grown. All produce is consumed domestically.

FORESTRY AND FISHING

Mongolia's forests yield timber for construction and for fuel. The timber harvest has increased significantly since the mid-1990s, and deforestation is beginning to affect both the forestry economy and the environment. Indigenous forest and steppe animals, such as marmots (a member of the squirrel family), squirrels, foxes, wolves, and deer, are hunted for their fur, meat, and other products. Animal hides are exported.

A very small fishing industry produces canned fish that is exported to several markets.

With the change to a market economy, herders who had relied for years on collectives to sell their produce are now facing difficulties; they must learn to sell in the open market, finding their own buyers.

MINING

Until the 1920s mining was limited to coal. The Nalaih mine near Ulaanbaatar is the country's oldest coal mine. Mongolia is rich not only in coal but also in copper, fluorspar, gold, iron ore, lead, tin, tungsten, and uranium. In the 1970s valuable deposits of copper, molybdenum, tin, tungsten, fluorspar, and gold were discovered, yet much of that remains to be exploited. Even so, Mongolia is a leading world producer and exporter of copper, molybdenum, and fluorspar. Mining is an important economic sector, accounting for more than 60 percent of the country's exports.

These young girls are collecting dried animal dung, which is a common form of fuel for many families.

ENERGY

Most of the country's coal is used to fuel power stations. Mongolia produces 6.2 million tons (5.6 million metric tons) of coal a year, a small slice of the country's reserve of at least 100 billion tons (91 billion metric tons).

Power stations are very visible in Ulaanbaatar and other towns. Most *aimag* centers have steam-driven thermal power plants or diesel generators. In the rural areas people still gather wood and dry animal dung to use as fuel, often the household chore of children.

Some coal is exported to Russia by rail in exchange for electricity. In 1995 fuel and energy made up more than 22 percent of imports. Mongolia is exploring alternative sources of fuel; it is prospecting for oil and gas, for example, and is developing wind and solar power.

Streets in Ulaanbaatar are normally filled with cars made in many countries, especially Japan and South Korea.

LIGHT INDUSTRY

Factories in Ulaanbaatar and Erdenet turn out carpets, knitwear, and products of cashmere wool (the cashmere goat's fine, soft undercoat), camel hair, and felt. Mongolia is the world's second-largest producer of cashmere. The food industry has meat-packing plants, dairies, and flour mills, and produces canned meat, sausages, butter, soap, and other commodities. There are also woodworking, paper, furniture, and construction enterprises that depend on the forestry industry.

CONSTRUCTION

The construction industry has been important in modernizing Mongolia. China provided the labor, materials, and expertise to help build brick and glass works, lumber mills, housing developments, and other projects. By the early 1990s, Mongolia had almost 100 national construction companies in operation.

There are brick, cement, and reinforced concrete plants, and timber mills in Ulaanbaatar, Darkhan, and other towns. Housing construction continues to keep pace with the increasing population.

TRANSPORTATION AND COMMUNICATIONS

Carts, drawn by horse, camel, or yak, have given way to modern road and rail transportation. Construction of the first hard-surface roads began in the late 1920s. In 1925 Mongolia established a state transportation committee with 12 trucks. Mongolia has about 30,600 miles (49,245 km) of roads, but only about 1,659 miles (2,670 km)—some 5.5 percent—are paved.

A Mongolian *ger*, or yurt, with satellite dish and solar panel, showing that traditional living can include high-tech conveniences, too.

Much of the development of modern transportation was done with Soviet aid, especially roads and bridges. Railroad construction began only in the late 1930s. The Trans-Mongolian Railway links Ulaanbaatar with Moscow in the north and Beijing in the southeast. Almost all of Mongolia's imports and exports are moved by rail.

Water transportation is minimal as Mongolia is landlocked. It has some 250 miles (400 km) of navigable waterways, mainly on Lake Hövsgöl and the Selenge River, used for carrying goods to and from Russia.

Air transportation is important because Mongolia's small population is spread over a very large area. Mongolian Airlines, or MIAT, the international carrier, runs a regular air service to most parts of the country and also provides crop-dusting services, forest and steppe air patrols, and air ambulance services—on top of carrying passengers, freight, and mail. There are 44 airports in Mongolia, including its one international airport near Ulaanbaatar. Mongolia has air links with Moscow, Beijing, Incheon, and Berlin as well as Seoul, Irkutsk, and Tokyo.

In 1921 the new revolutionary government nationalized postal and telecommunication services that had been Russian-, Chinese-, and Danish-owned, and established a Mongolian postal and telegraph department. Soviet aid helped Mongolia develop its communication networks.

In the 13th century Mongolia had a sophisticated communications system of horse relay. All herders had to contribute horses to this system. Horse relay stations, or örtöö (OOR-taw), were maintained at intervals of 20 to 30 miles (32 to 48 km) along the main routes crossing the Mongol Empire. A court messenger could arrive at any station and be assured of being fed and rested as well as receiving a fresh mount for the rest of his journey.

Marco Polo wrote, "Whatever route the messenger took from the capital . . . he would arrive at an örtöö, each of which maintained some 300 to 400 horses, always ready to take the messenger on. There are premises for accommodating and lodging the messengers, and every other thing they might require."

The örtöö system was like the Pony Express that linked the western United States with the developed eastern states from 1860 to 1861, although the Pony Express was mainly a mail service with stations 25 to 75 miles (40 to 120 km) apart. Unlike the Pony Express riders, who handed their saddlebags to another rider at the next relay station, the Mongolian couriers rode the full distance themselves, often covering 50 to 70 miles (80 to 113 km) a day, stopping only briefly if at all for food and rest. They would strap themselves up tightly with leather belts to keep from falling off their horses if they dozed in the saddle.

The örtöö system helped to build and administer the Mongol Empire by providing quick and efficient communication between the khan and his far-ranging army. It remained in operation until the early 20th century. In 1913 there were still 150 stations on the main roads that passed through the capital and crossed the country from north to south and from east to west, an effective web.

Communication infrastructure in Mongolia has grown remarkably in the last decade. The country now counts over 46,000 Internet subscribers, 320,000 Internet users, more than 20 Internet providers, 80,000 households with cable TV, 68 television broadcast stations, 148,200 (2008) main telephone lines in use, and about 2 million (2008) mobile cellular phone subscribers.

Many youths in Mongolia have enthusiastically adopted the Internet.

BANKING AND FINANCIAL SERVICES

Until 1924 Mongolia did not have any banks of its own—or a currency, either. There was an active barter trade, using livestock, tea, and salt. Within the country, Russian and Chinese currencies were used, while foreign trade was in U.S. dollars and the British pound. Most of the banks that existed at the time were owned by Chinese business interests.

The revolutionary government reformed the system and established the Mongolbank (now known as the Bank of Mongolia) in 1924. A year later the government introduced the *tögrög* (TOOG-roog) as the national currency. All debts to moneylenders and foreign merchants were canceled, and private lending was outlawed. All state enterprises had to deposit their money with the state bank, which controlled all financial transactions in the country.

FOREIGN TRADE

Before the 1990s Mongolia's main trading partners were the Soviet Union and the East European countries. Trade with other communist countries increased after Mongolia joined the Council for Mutual Economic Assistance (COMECON) in 1962.

Until the 1980s Mongolia continued to import more than it exported; the Soviet Union was its major trading partner. In 2007 Mongolia imported most

Mongolia joined the Group of 77 in 1989; the International Monetary Fund, World Bank, and Asian Development Bank in 1991; and the World Trade Organization in 1997.

Many Mongolians dislike the rigid discipline and schedules of the urban workplace. They are used to a lifestyle of freedom of movement and work that follows the seasons, reflecting their ancient nomadic behavior.

of its goods from China, Russia, South Korea, and Japan. The main imports are machinery, fuel, cars, food products, and industrial consumer goods. The main export markets are China, Canada, and the United States. Mongolia exports mainly mineral products and textiles.

WORKERS

With economic development, the labor force has grown dramatically—from 1960 to 1983 the number of workers doubled. Today almost half of all workers are engaged in material production. Most of them have had eight to nine years of schooling. Mongolians generally work an eight-hour day and enjoy 15 days of paid vacation a year.

The majority of Mongolia's workforce, more than 61 percent, is in the service sector. About 33 percent is in agriculture, and approximately 5 percent is in the industrial sector.

Closure of state enterprises caused a large increase in unemployment in the cities, which peaked in 2003 at around 20—25 percent but has since recovered astonishingly to a rate of 2.8 percent. Despite this betterment, the number of poor in the country is still over 1 million, consisting of more than 36 percent of the population.

TOURISM INDUSTRY

The tourism industry of Mongolia is of major importance, as it makes up over 18 percent of the annual gross domestic product. The last decade has seen an explosion in the number of tour agencies and hotels, from cheap dormitory-style accommodations to fancy four-star hotels such as the Ulaanbaatar and the Chinggis Khan.

The mountains attract climbers, and tourists come to enjoy other outdoor activities, including skiing and ice-skating, camping, hiking, fishing, riding, and kayaking. There are tourist *gers,* too, so the visitor can get a taste of living Mongolian style.

The three main tourist centers are Terelj, northeast of Ulaanbaatar; Hujirt in the southwest; and the Gobi Desert center.

THE MONGOLIAN STOCK EXCHANGE

The Mongolian Stock Exchange (MSE) was created in 1991 as part of the country's program to privatize state-owned companies and develop a capital market. From 1992 to 1995 there was free distribution of vouchers to all Mongolian citizens for buying shares in companies on the state exchange. Then, starting in August 1995, the MSE began functioning as a regular stock exchange, with a listing of 470 companies. The Mongolian Securities Commission, created in 1995, is charged with regulating and controlling activities in the securities market.

The majestic Chinggis Khan Hotel in Ulaanbaatar.

TOWARD A MARKET ECONOMY

The change to a market economy caused an economic crisis in the early 1990s with the collapse of trade and foreign aid ties with the former Soviet Union. Industrial production dropped because of fuel shortages and distribution problems, and basic foodstuffs had to be rationed. Inflation was 325 percent in 1992. After the opposition came to power in 1996, wide-ranging economic reforms were implemented. Government spending was cut, insolvent banks were closed, utility prices raised, and foreign investment welcomed. Inflation dropped to 35 percent, and a four-year economic program was announced that allowed more private ownership of state property.

Mongolia's economy saw rapid growth between 2004 and 2008, spurred mainly by high copper prices and increased gold production. This in turn caused inflation to skyrocket to over 40 percent. The weakening global economy in 2008 started to lower the inflation rate significantly, but it is taking a toll on Mongolia's exports.

ENVIRONMENT

The Darhat depression located
at the end of the Mongol steppe.

CHAPTER 5

MONGOLIA'S ENVIRONMENTAL story is a mix of good news and bad news. Deforestation, desertification, and air and water pollution are some of the serious problems facing Mongolia as it seeks its place among developing countries in the 21st century. Traditionally a pastoral and nomadic people, Mongolians are finding that progress, when measured with such yardsticks as gross domestic product and industrial output and trade, has a high price tag.

Rock formations by the Terkhiin Tsagaan Nuur Lake (White Lake) in the Khangai Mountains of Mongolia.

The Gobi Desert has been one of the most prolific sources of fossil finds in the world. There the first ever dinosaur egg was found. The Gobi is also home to many rare species of both plants and animals. But the increasingly rapid spread of the desert is threatening Mongolia and China alike.

Mongolia's environment has suffered from its people's need to catch up with the rest of the world by hastily transitioning from a traditional mode of life to an unfamiliar one that is more up-to-date. Abruptness is the bad news. The good news is that Mongolia is now learning from the environmental mistakes made. There are now laws and better controls that try correcting such adverse effects of progress. The government, with the help of international agencies, monitors and enforces new regulations, keeping a sharp eye fixed on the environment.

Shrubbery such as these veterans have survived the harsh conditions of the Gobi Desert of Mongolia.

A FRAGILE PLACE

Mongolia is in the center of the Asian continent, and much of its land is in high altitude. Its climate is harsh, cold, and dry for much of the year. The summer season is short, making the growing of crops always difficult. Mongolia gets very little rain. Most of the rain falls in the northern parts of the country during a three-month period in the summer. Ulaanbaatar receives an average of 9 inches (220 mm) of rain, compared with only 4 inches (102 mm) in the south. Mongolia has an annual average rainfall ranging between 8 and 9 inches (200 and 220 mm), far less than that falling on the state of California (16 inches, or over 400 mm) and just barely more than what Arizona receives (6 inches or about 140 mm). The country endures regular droughts every two or three years. Its southern regions are very dry and are covered by semidesert or desert land. Its latitude, the generally high altitude of the land, and its location in the middle of the continent result in extreme temperatures; winter temperatures are low and freezing over much of the country. As a result, the soil is thin and the ecosystem is fragile and easily disturbed.

THE PRESSURE OF PROGRESS

In the past, Mongolians lived in accordance with what the land and climate would allow. Their traditional lifestyle has been shaped by the nature of their country. But in the 1950s there began a move to change the nomadic, pastoral, and somewhat agricultural economy to one that was to be more industrial. In order to make Mongolia more developed and progressive, the government pushed for intensive agriculture and industrialization by exploiting the rich mineral resources, speeding up urbanization, and encouraging rapid economic development. Little thought was given to planning, managing the fragile environment, or ensuring the renewability of resources.

Statistically speaking, more than three-quarters of the land (292 million acres or 118 million hectares) is used for agriculture and animal husbandry, giving the misleading impression that much of the country is highly productive. A closer look at the numbers, however, shows that only a very small proportion of this area (2.5 million acres or 1 million ha) is agricultural.

The best arable land is found in the northern *aimags* of Tov and Selenge, where nearly 60 percent of the country's agriculture takes place. The rest is best employed as pastureland because animal husbandry requires lots of land on which livestock can graze and move along. It is mountainous and consists

Arable and fertile plains such as these are threatened by the rapid expansion of agricultural industries.

Soil erosion of the Gobi Desert, contributing to the expansion of the enormous hostile area.

of grass and desert steppelands; consequently, less than 10 percent of the remaining area is under cultivation. These lands have always been more suited to the grazing of animals, which is why the vast flowing steppes and rolling hills of Mongolia have been home to countless generations of nomadic herdsmen and their families. The Gobi Desert in the south is barren and inhospitable to human economic activity and, furthermore, is growing by nearly 1,400 square miles (3,626 square km) each year.

DESERTIFICATION AND DEFORESTATION

Bad farming practices and overgrazing of the steppes have caused the rapid deterioration of the land. Between 1960 and 1989, the area that was taken under cultivation increased greatly. Wheat became the main crop grown. There was intensive tilling of the raw land with little or no attention given to protecting the soil. This caused erosion and deterioration of the soil quality, resulting in reduced fertility of the small amount of arable land that Mongolia has and leading to the abandonment of much of the vast wheat fields.

As with farming, poor animal husbandry practices contributed to the desertification of the land. Herders became increasingly more settled and tended to roam less. That resulted in pastures being overgrazed, especially since the herds of animals had grown larger. Since 1990, the number of cattle near Ulaanbaatar has doubled, thanks in part to the privatization of the herds and the growth spurt in human population. Pasturelands, especially around the capital, became seriously overgrazed. The lack of good pasture led to poorer quality of animals and related products. Like the bad farming practices, overgrazing caused soil erosion and the thinning out of the steppe grasses.

A third factor in the process of desertification was deforestation. The move to a free market economy in the 1990s was hard on Mongolia's forests. Rapid privatization of land ownership, a lack of effective governmental oversight, and an increase in the demand for timber (for fuel and for the building and woodworking industries) caused an unsustainable jump in the size of timber harvests. Overall, the area of Mongolia's forests has been reduced by 12 percent since 1990. As the trees are cut down or are lost to forest fires and insect damage, the resulting deforestation contributes to more soil erosion. Trees, plants, and grasses together provide protection for the soil from the sun and the wind. They stabilize the soil with their roots, shade the earth, prevent moisture from being sucked up by the intense heat of the sun, and break the force of the wind that stirs up dust storms.

Hikers enjoy the lush green hills and deep blue 100-mile-long lake found at Hövsgöl National Park in northern Mongolia.

Climate change, which is affecting the whole earth, is another contributing factor to desertification. In Mongolia this global phenomenon has caused a gradual reduction in the country's annual rainfall, further accelerating soil erosion.

WATER AND AIR POLLUTION

Mongolia's environmental problems do not stop at desertification and deforestation. The country's air and water quality have also suffered from the impact of increased economic activity and a fast-growing population. In the 1990s Mongolia's population growth rate was one of the highest in Asia, at 2.7 percent per year. But this has decreased somewhat, with the population growth rate for 2009 estimated at 1.49 percent. More than half of Mongolia's population, not long ago a very rural people, now lives in urban centers. While the majority of people in towns and cities have access to clean drinking water, people living in rural areas are not as fortunate. In 2000, 77

Lake Hovsgol in northern Mongolia contains around 70 percent of the nation's total reservoir of freshwater. The 85-mile- (137-km-) long crystal clear mountain lake supports a large and diverse ecosystem that is mainly undisturbed by humans, thanks to its remote location and harsh winter climate.

percent of the urban population and only 30 percent of the rural population had access to clean drinking water. Even today many rural families have to draw water in buckets from village wells and carry it back to their homes. Housing, transportation, solid and liquid waste-management facilities, and other infrastructure development have not kept pace with the growing demands of a larger population and economic development.

Water quality is a constant problem, due in large part to the relative lack of proper sewerage systems and water-treatment facilities. Poor housing in urban areas, rapid industrialization, and economic development without adequate controls have resulted in the contamination of the air, water, soil, and groundwater. The rapid rise in the demand for water has caused an ominous drop in lake and river water and in groundwater levels.

The single biggest source of water pollution in Mongolia comes from irresponsible mining and petroleum extraction practices. Until very recently, these activities were done with little government regulation. If there were regulatory laws, they were very poorly enforced. Companies extracting oil did not pay much attention to the risk of oil leaching into the ground. Many mines dumped their wastes wherever it was easiest and cheapest, even if it was close to freshwater sources that could become contaminated. Outdated mining techniques and equipment involved the heavy use of chemicals such as mercury and cyanide. This meant that there was a great risk that these toxic chemicals and the oil might leach into the groundwater supply.

A dramatic waterfall in the Orhon Valley of Mongolia.

The leather industry is another culprit for water pollution. Leather, mostly produced near the capital, Ulaanbaatar, requires large quantities of chemicals such as lime, ammonium chloride, sodium sulfide, and various sulfates in the tanning process. The highly alkaline combination of lime and sodium sulfide is dangerous to workers who are preparing the leather and is often simply washed down the drain or dumped on the ground. This tanning waste, which makes up nearly half of the total waste from leather processing, gradually finds its way into the ground, contaminating enormous quantities of groundwater.

Smoke from industrial factories contributes to the air pollution problem in Mongolia.

The problem with air quality is concentrated mainly in the urban areas. The air in towns and cities is polluted largely by the coal and wood fuel used by power plants, industries, cooking and heating stoves of individual dwellings, and by the dirty engine emissions of vehicles. Mongolia experiences annual periods of very low wind and wide temperature fluctuations from late fall to early spring. During these periods the high levels of particulates in the air frequently reach proportions that are hazardous to health and put young children and the elderly at risk of lethal respiratory illnesses.

AN ACTION PLAN

In 1993 Mongolia initiated a National Environmental Action Plan outlining steps to ensure that environmental concerns would be linked to the country's overall economic and social development. Architects of the plan looked at the environmental situation and worked out how Mongolia could manage

A musk deer thrives freely in the wild, though its future is endangered by illegal hunting.

its natural resources, deal with its pollution and environmental hazards, and conserve its natural heritage. Mongolia's Ministry for Nature and Environment got much-needed help from international environmental specialists to assess and monitor their action plan.

Mongolia is slowly starting to see improvements being made across the country. Land regulations were introduced in 1995 and 2000. New land-management techniques have been introduced with the help of the World Bank and its associated international agencies such as the International Development Association. For instance, the planting of trees around agricultural lands has been encouraged to reduce soil erosion caused by wind. With a growing national awareness of Mongolia's environmental problems, the situation is improving. The government recognizes that there are many unique features of the country that need to be safeguarded. Forest and wildlife preserves have thus been created and endangered animal species are now protected by law and public education.

The National Environmental Action Plan hopefully will take Mongolia well into the 21st century, with economic development happening at a pace commensurate with what the land can sustain.

WILDLIFE MANAGEMENT

Mongolia is made up of one of the most varied mixes of climatic zones of any Asian nation, all within a relatively small area about the size of Alaska. These zones include flood plains, forests, tundra, taiga, salty marshes, freshwater sources, steppes, semidesert, and the fifth-largest desert area in the world. This diversity has made Mongolia home to numerous animal species, including 139 types of mammals, 449 varieties of birds, 76 kinds of fish, 22 reptile species, and 6 different amphibians.

The wild fauna has to compete with domesticated herds for pasture and water. In the last 20 years, a very significant increase in the size of Mongolian livestock herds has threatened to overwhelm the capabilities of the land to support them. These herds of goats, sheep, and cattle eat up ever widening swaths of grassland, leaving slim pickings for the much smaller, more dispersed groups of wild ungulates such as deer.

The growing human population of Mongolia is also creating new communities that impact on the land. There are many more people journeying through areas once roamed only by small groups of nomads. The frequent droughts and the long dry season, combined with the carelessness of the people, have caused an increase in the numbers of forest and grass fires, harming the habitat of the Mongolian gazelles, roe deer, red deer, and musk deer.

Sadly, many of these animal species are in danger of becoming extinct. Rare species, such as the musk deer, are being threatened by a decadelong increase in illegal hunting. The hunting is done partially by herdsmen seeking variety in their diet, but mainly by poachers who make a quick profit selling rare animal organs and other parts on the black market.

The rare and endangered snow leopard can still be found in the nature reserves of Mongolia.

These predatory groups are often well organized and heavily armed, making it very hard for the Mongolian border guards and park rangers to deal with them. Moreover, lack of funds makes it difficult to hire and train enough staff to maintain the parks, fend off poachers, and enforce pollution laws.

On a more positive note, the government has increased the number of protected areas and nature preserves. Since 1992, the number of areas declared as protected or as national reserves or parklands has more than tripled. These areas now encompass more than 14 percent of the total land area of Mongolia.

The Great Gobi Strict Protected Area is Mongolia's largest and probably most important preserve. At over 20,500 square miles (53,095 square km), the Great Gobi area includes both arid and semiarid land, ranging from vast plains and narrow valleys to rugged mountain ranges. The Great Gobi is home to over 410 species of plants, 150 species of birds, 15 different species of reptiles and amphibians, and 49 species of mammals. The dry and rocky area contains some of the rarest species of animals on the planet, including the world's only desert bear, the Gobi bear (*Ursus arctos gobiensis*), the wild Przewalski's horse, and Mongolia's last remaining wild Bactrian camels. The Great Gobi has been nominated for UNESCO World Heritage recognition.

Other notable parks and protected zones include the Gorkhi-Terelj National Park, famed for its rock-climbing areas, the Yestii hot spring, and the Uvs Nuur Strictly Protected Area, which is made up of four separate sections: Uvs Nuur, Tiirgen Uul, Tsagaan Shuvuut, and Altal Els. Together these four areas represent nearly every type of climate in Mongolia from deserts to snowfields and from forests to marshlands. The park is also home to numerous rare and endangered species such as the snow leopard (*Uncia uncia Schreber*).

Wetlands at the Gurvan Saikhan National Park, an example of the extreme diversification in the Gobi Desert.

PRZEWALSKI'S HORSE (*EQUUS FERUS PRZEWALSKII*)

Named for Russian colonel, explorer, and naturalist Nikolai Przhevalskii, who led an expedition in 1881 to find it, Przewalski's horse is the last true wild horse in the world. Unlike its "wild" cousins, such as the American mustang, which is actually a domesticated horse gone feral, the Przewalski has never been domesticated. The short, stocky horses typically stand at around 13 hands (52 inches, or 1.33 m) and are 20.6 hands (83 inches, or 2.1 m) in length, with a 35-inch (89-cm) tail, and have pale brown flanks, a yellowish white belly, and a stiff, dark brown mane.

By 1969 these horses, also known as the Asian wild horse, the Mongolian wild horse, or the Takhi, had become extinct in the wild. At that time, the only remaining Przewalski's horses left in the world were in two sites, a zoo in the German city of Munich, and another in the Czech city of Prague. Both populations were based on animals captured in the early 1900s.

Nearly 30 years after the last Przewalski's horse was spotted in the wild, these wonderful animals are returning. Sixteen horses were reintroduced into Mongolia in 1992, and amazingly the breed appears to be thriving. Though still critically endangered, the population has grown to over 248 in the wild in Mongolia and to more than 1,500 in reserves and zoos around the world. With careful management and protection, the last true wild horse in the world may once again become a common sight on the vast steppes of Mongolia.

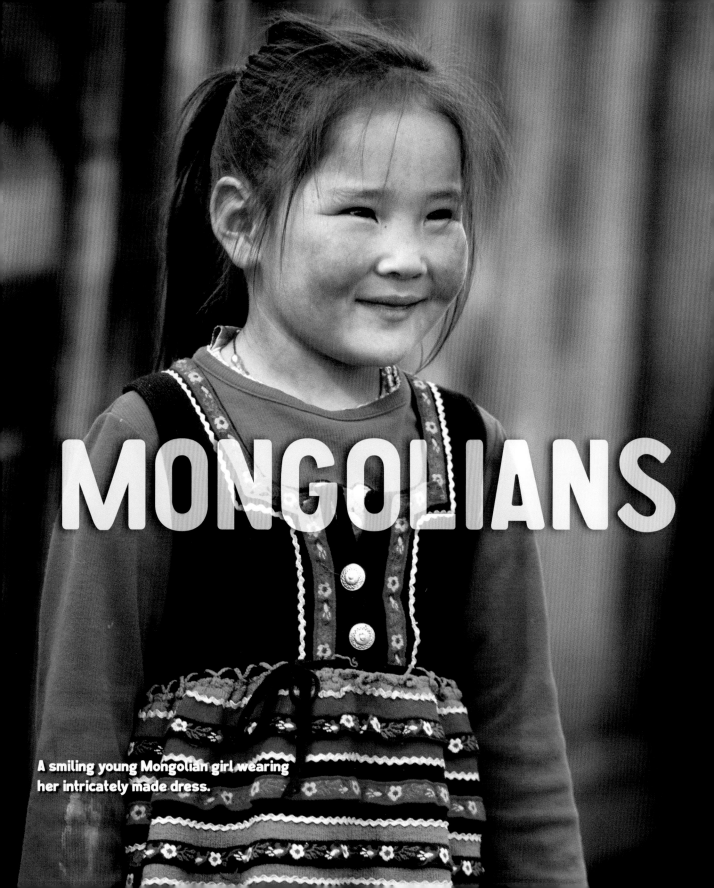

MONGOLIANS

A smiling young Mongolian girl wearing her intricately made dress.

MONGOLIA IS ONE OF THE most sparsely populated countries in the world and has an uneven population distribution. The most densely populated regions are the river valleys of forested mountain slopes and the grasslands; the least populated areas are the desert, semidesert, and mountainous regions.

Mongolians are a largely unknown people, because during most of its history the country was closed to the Western world. The brief exception to its insularity was during the 13th century, when the Mongol Empire was at its strongest. What was known about the Mongols was mixed with fable and fear. Mongolia is now more open and accessible.

Despite their Western-style clothing, most young Mongolians retain their traditional love of brightly colored outfits.

CHAPTER 6

The medical terms "mongolism" or "mongoloid" were once used to describe people with Down syndrome. Such people were thought to resemble Mongolians. Those terms are now inappropriate and offensive to both Mongolians and people with Down syndrome.

63

Mongolia is a fast-growing society. Since the early 1920s, improvements in health care and living standards have made it possible for the population to increase quite rapidly. Just before the revolution, there were only about half a million people. Today, the population has increased more than sixfold, a growth rate significantly higher than the rest of the world. The growth rate peaked at 2.6 percent in 1992 but has since declined to a still significant 1.49 percent. As a result, Mongolia has a very young society. In 2008 over one-third of the population was under 15 years of age, and two-thirds of the population was under the age of 30.

As the country continues to modernize and industrialize, the migration of people from rural areas to the cities is also expected to increase. In 2008 the proportion of rural to urban inhabitants was 43 percent to 57 percent respectively.

Family size in Mongolia has seen a drop from an average of 5 people per household to just over 3 in urban areas and just over 3.5 in rural ones. Better health care has also increased the life expectancy of the average Mongolian man to 65 years and of the average woman to 70 years. There used to be more men than women, but today there is an almost equal proportion of men and women in the population.

ETHNIC GROUPS

There are two main ethnic groups: the Mongolian group and the Turkic group. The majority of the people fall into the Mongolian group.

Of this group, 70 percent are the nomadic Khalkha Mongols who live mainly in the eastern and central part of the country. The word *khalkha* (HAL-ha), meaning shield, originated around the 17th century when the various clans of Mongols of the east formed an alliance in their struggle against the Manchu, or Qing, dynasty of China.

The other peoples in the Mongolian group are the Döröd, Buriat, Barga, Üzem-chin, Darhad, Zahchin, Bayad, Myangat, Dariganga, Ööld, Torguut, Harchin, Tsahar, and Hotgon. These Mongols live mainly in the west and northwest and along the southeast border with China.

The differences among these groups and their dialects are small, so they understand each other easily. Their ethnic clothing varies only slightly from group to group, perhaps simply in the kind of headdress worn or in the shape of the shoes.

The second ethnic group are the Turkic people, or Kazakhs, who make up 6 percent of the population. They are pastoral people, traditionally Muslim, and they live mainly in the Altai region situated in the extreme western part of the country. They are renowned hunters who pursue their quarry on horseback and use trained golden eagles and greyhounds to attack prey. Many Kazakhs work in the coal mines of north-central Mongolia. Tuvinians, Urianhai, and Uighurs are all Turkic peoples.

A small number of Russians and Chinese live permanently in Mongolia. In the early 1920s, many Chinese in Mongolia were merchants, traders, and artisans who worked in the Buddhist monasteries. Many Russians came to Mongolia as advisers and skilled workers during the communist period, married Mongol women, had children, and became assimilated into the local population.

Kazakh nomads living in the Uvs province of Mongolia.

It is estimated that by the end of the year 2009 the population of Mongolia will have passed 3 million.

A FEUDAL SOCIETY

Young monks receiving an education in a Buddhist monastery.

Before the 1921 revolution, Mongolian culture was a fixed feudal society with no social mobility. At the top were the lords claiming descent from Genghis Khan. The commoners worked for the feudal lords, herding their livestock and doing military service when called to it.

There was very little formal education, and it was difficult to change one's status in society. The only "escape" route was through the Buddhist monasteries. Young boys and men might offer their service to the monasteries where, by choosing a monastic career, they could get an education. From the waning of the empire in the 16th century to the beginning of the 20th century, the influence of the Lamaist Buddhist religion resulted in almost half of the male population becoming monks. The lamas, or monks, were a politically and socially powerful class in feudal Mongolian society, but their influence was curbed when the communists came to power in the 1920s.

Most of the population, about 90 percent, were common serfs and lowly monks. The aristocrats, who formed about 8 percent of the population, were the political leaders and administrators.

SOCIETY IS REVOLUTIONIZED

The structure of Mongolian society underwent major changes after the revolution, as feudalism was seen as contrary to communism.

Power and wealth were stripped away from the feudal lords and the powerful monasteries and were redistributed among the people. Mongolian herders, who used to be self-sufficient, were organized into herding collectives or attached to state factories and mines. These herding collectives have now ceased to exist. A monetary system was introduced, and people earned wages for their work. They were supervised by a new class of managers and administrators belonging to the Mongolian People's Revolutionary Party.

Much emphasis was placed on planning, projects, and meeting goals and targets. Everything was done for the collective good of society. Workers and their units competed to do a job quickly or surpass a production quota. They received benefits such as free medical care, education, and pensions when they retired. Those who excelled at their jobs were honored as "number one" workers. Most working people were party members.

A formal education became important, and most young Mongolians were enrolled in schools where they also learned the new party ideology. They were taught punctuality, rules and standards, and the totally novel need to meet production goals.

The bureaucrats and high-ranking party members were the elite. Next came the professionals—technicians, engineers, doctors, and others. These citizens had access to post-secondary education. Then there were the administrators and workers in the factories and on state farms. Living on the fringes were the traditional nomadic herders whose livelihood depended on the weather and health of their animals, and the performance of their new herding collective.

A mix of the old-style marketplace and modern city living can be seen at the Khar Zakh (Black Market) in Ulaanbaatar.

COLORFUL ROBES

The traditional garment for both Mongolian men and women is a long, flowing robe tied at the waist by a sash. It looks much like a dressing gown that is fastened from the throat and down the right shoulder by small cloth buttons. It has a small stand-up collar. This gown is called the *del*.

Beneath the *del*, Mongolians wear heavy trousers that are tucked into leather or felt knee-high boots with pointed toes. These boots are worn several sizes too large so that as the weather gets colder, thick socks of wool, felt, or fur can be used to pad the boots, keeping the wearer's feet warm and comfortable. Russian army boots are also very popular.

Both the *del*, which reaches down to below the knees, and the sash are often very colorful. The *del* is commonly worn in rural areas. In the winter it has an inner lining of sheepskin or red fox fur that keeps the wearer warm. The colors and shapes of *dels* differ according to the different ethnic groups of the wearers.

Mongolian men and women in traditional robes, the colorful *dels*.

Dashdorjin Natsagdorj (1906—37) is considered the father of contemporary Mongolian literature. Most Mongolians know by heart his famous poem "My Motherland," portraying Mongolia as an old country renewed with a glorious future. The "Four Seasons of the Year" is about building a new Mongolia. The poem "Star" explores the possibility of flights into space. Natsagdorj was also a playwright and the author of Three Tragic Fates, *the first Mongolian opera.*

Balduugiyn Sharav (1869—1939), a celebrated painter, spent his childhood in a monastery and later traveled all over Mongolia. The frequent subjects of his paintings were the simple life and traditions of the people. He used traditional techniques. One Day in the Life of Mongolia, *his masterpiece, is full of intricate drawings depicting many aspects of Mongolian life.*

In the summer men sometimes wear a Western-style felt hat or Russian-style cap; in the winter, a warmer fur cap with earflaps is worn to keep the ears warm.

City people, especially office workers, are more often seen in Western-style outfits. The women wear dresses and the men dull-colored shirts, suits, and shoes. Almost everybody, however, has a special festive *del* reserved for formal occasions.

The young people in Mongolian towns are like their contemporaries in other cities in the world. Boys love wearing jeans, shirts, and jackets; the girls wear dresses.

The hair of the women is long and often braided or coiled at the back of the head.

When a Mongol woman gets married, she is dressed in traditional finery that usually includes an extremely elaborate headdress and heavy jewelry made from silver and semiprecious stones. The style of the headdress varies from one ethnic group to another.

Ornately adorned Mongolian women in their festival costumes.

LIFESTYLE

Local men sawing planks in a lumberyard.

MONGOLIANS VALUE THE freedom of open movement that is characteristic of a nomadic life. It's no surprise that the practice of pastoralism is still important in Mongolian life. It shapes the way Mongolians generally see the world. They love the countryside and have a close affinity with nature, which has such a major effect on their daily lives, and with their animals, with which they have an interdependent, or symbiotic, relationship. Even young Mongolians living in the cities go out to the countryside as often as they can to touch a part of their heritage.

Mongolians have a saying, "*Erhuni jargal, idsugui heer,*" meaning, "Man's joy is in wide-open and empty spaces."

A young herder checking his sheep in a pen.

The modern
Mongol family is
usually a nuclear
one, with parents,
children, and
sometimes a
grandparent.

THE MODERN NOMAD

Traditional livestock herding has been modernized. Horses are still important but are supplemented with jeeps, trucks, and motorcycles. Herders can get the latest weather reports and storm warnings on radio. At winter camps, portable power generators provide energy.

The old herding collectives often had the same boundaries as their district's administrative center. The centers provide services to the herders and their families: a school, storage facilities, movies, health facilities, a machinery repair station, and offices. The average household owns a television set, a radio, a sewing machine, a bicycle, and a motorcycle or a truck.

A herding camp has two to six households, sometimes related families, managing the livestock together. A family can be part of one camp one year and move on to another the next, though some families remain with one camp for a long time. Herders do not own any grazing ground, but there is an understanding that each camp has the right to use certain areas.

During the summer months herds are moved over a vast area to places with good grazing land and abundant water. In the wintertime the camp moves to a site where there is water, dried grass, and shelter from storms. Weaker animals not expected to survive the harsh winter are killed in the late fall to reduce the herd size. The meat is dried and stored for the winter when neither sheep nor horses produce milk.

A modern Mongolian nomad using a cell phone outside his *ger*.

FIVE IMPORTANT ANIMALS

Mongolians have always depended for their well-being on five animals—horses, camels, sheep, cattle or yaks, and goats. These are known as "the five snouts, or muzzles, of livestock" and appear in every aspect of Mongolian life, art, and literature. Not every herder has all five, but many have more than one type. The horse is the most important. It is seldom used as a draft animal, but is ridden. It also provides such products as the alcoholic drink *airag*, horsehair rope, and horsehide leather. Apart from the meat, milk, and other dairy products, dried dung of the various animals is used as fuel. Leather goods are made from the hides. In the mountains the yak, a hardy type of ox, is particularly useful. Camels are beasts of burden in the desert and are used for transportation. Sheep's and goat's wool are used for winter clothing and for making the felt that is used to cover the *ger*. The men and boys look after the horses, while the women tend the other animals.

THE *GER*

Mongolians traditionally live in a dome-shaped structure called a *ger*, also called a yurt. Its portability makes it ideal for a nomadic lifestyle. Although apartment buildings are found in cities, most Mongolians in the countryside and small towns still live in *gers*. Even in Ulaanbaatar, the capital, clusters

A legend regarding the *ger* tells that the first Mongol was born after a fair-haired man came through the opening at the top and impregnated Alan-gua, the mother of the Mongols. In the nomadic society of the Mongolians, a community is based on helping one another. It is said that the *ger* door is seldom locked even when the family is out. Any weary traveler can enter to warm himself by the fire, have a rest, and take some food. For the nomads, a visitor is very welcome as days on the steppes can be very long and lonely.

of *gers* dot the outskirts. A city *ger* often has electricity, while one in the country depends on candles and lamps for lighting.

A large brick or metal stove for heat and cooking stands in the middle, its stovepipe rising through a roof vent. At the sides of the *ger* there may be some low, steel-framed beds curtained off. There are large decorated storage chests for clothing and other items, and a few mirrors, photographs, and religious pictures hang on the walls. A low table and some small metal folding chairs occupy the space around the stove. The wooden floor is covered with rugs. The man's working tools, his saddle, and the leather bag containing *airag* are on his side on the left, under the sky god's protection; the kitchen and cooking utensils are on the woman's side on the right, under the sun's protection. The back of the *ger* is reserved for elders, honored guests, and the family altar. The posts symbolize the link with heaven; it is bad manners to lean against them. A little bag holding herbs to ward off evil spirits is hung from the top. Mongolians never stand or step on the threshold of the door but step over it.

An inside view of a traditional Mongolian *ger*, a normad's cozy, portable house.

ERECTING A *GER*

The wooden floor of the ger is assembled first. Next, the lattice walls are joined end to end to form the lower, circular part of the ger, and the door, which always faces south, is put in place. The walls are made of thin wooden strips fastened in a crisscross lattice, enabling the wall to be opened and shut like a concertina. The size of the ger depends on the number of lattice walls; there may be up to 12 walls in a large structure.

When the circular wall is finished, two wooden posts are set up in the middle of the floor. The small wooden wheel forming the opening in the roof is carefully balanced on them. Long roof poles, painted orange like the sun, are inserted into slots on the wheel so that they radiate from the center like the ribs of a big umbrella. Then the lower ends of the poles are attached to the lattice walls with leather loops. A layer of canvas is stretched tightly over the roof. Thickly padded felt curtains are hung from the walls for insulation. Then, layer upon layer of felt is spread on the roof. In the winter, more felt layers are piled on. Finally, the whole structure is covered with white canvas to keep out the rain. The hole at the top is covered by a small triangle of canvas, adjusted by cords from the floor. It can be opened to let in light and air and allow smoke to leave, or closed in bad weather. A second, smaller ger may be erected for extra storage space.

The average weight of a ger without furniture is about 550 pounds (250 kg). It takes about an hour and a half to erect it. When the family moves, the ger is taken down and placed on a cart pulled by yaks, camels, or horses or, nowadays, perhaps on a pickup truck.

MAKING FELT

Felt is a very important product to Mongolians; it is used to cover the ger and to make rugs, saddle pads, and the linings of boots. Felt is made in the fall, and practically everyone takes part in making it. The material is usually made from sheep's wool, as wool fibers have minute barblike scales that interlock when they are processed.

The wool is first beaten to clean and loosen the fibers and to mix them up. A very large piece of old felt is placed on the ground and wet Then three layers of wool are carefully spread on top of it, as evenly as possible, and the wool is drenched with water. A layer of grass is sprinkled across the top.

Next, the four layers (the old felt with the three layers of new wool) are tightly rolled up around a pole—the grass sprinkled on top prevents the new wool from sticking together. The roll is thoroughly saturated again, then wrapped in leather and tied with leather thongs. Loops at the ends of the pole are attached by ropes to horses. Two riders on horses roll the bundle back and forth until the fibers of the new wool interlock and are tightly compressed, forming new felt.

When the roll is unfurled, the new felt is watered down once more and then allowed to dry beneath the sun. The wetting and drying process and the rolling shrinks the felt, making it dense and durable.

ROLE OF WOMEN

Women are about half the population. In the traditional nomadic society still found in rural areas, women help to milk, feed, and look after the animals, especially when they give birth to their young. They prepare and cook the meat and dairy products and grind the grain. Their important contribution to the functioning of the household gives them status, and they have a say in family matters. The constitution guarantees equal rights with men. Abortion was legalized in 1989.

Before the revolution women could not choose their husbands nor could they divorce them; they were completely dependent. After the revolution women were welcomed to every kind of education. They could work outside their homes and earn a living, and they could vote. Pregnant women received special benefits at work, in line with the government policy of encouraging larger families. Mongolian women found work as teachers, nurses, doctors, technicians, factory workers, and businesswomen.

With the changeover to a market economy in the 1990s, women were the more severely affected. When state-run factories closed and government departments cut wages and reduced their staffs, more women than men lost jobs and income. The social-support and health-care systems that had allowed women to work were curtailed, child-care facilities became expensive or were closed, and maternity benefits were reduced.

A number of organizations promote the women's movement, legal issues, equal opportunities for work, and better health care. The Mongolian Women's Federation, the oldest women's organization in the country, has more than 30 organizations as members. The Mongolian's Federation of Business and Professional Women was established in 1992.

Mongolian women working in a cashmere wool factory in Ulaanbaatar.

Marmots are very useful for medicinal purposes. Marmot oil is good for burns. For a problem with the left kidney, part of the left kidney of the marmot is eaten raw.

GETTING MARRIED IN MONGOLIA

The process of getting married used to be a long, drawn-out affair that took from one to three years and involved matchmakers and the giving of dowries.

An offer was first made by the groom's parents through a matchmaker. After the prospective bride's parents gave a positive reply, both families visited a lama to set a propitious date. Ten days later the groom's father and the matchmaker called on the bride's parents with an offering of ceremonial blue silk cloth. Six months after the date was set, the groom visited his intended, and a small party was organized. Six months after the party, gifts were exchanged. On the wedding day the groom took the bride away to her new home, a new *ger* built by the groom near the bride's *ger*. The bride's first duty was to make tea for the guests; then the festivities began.

Most modern Mongolians choose their own partner, marry at the Wedding Palace or state marriage registry, and later celebrate with a feast. Divorces are not common, but the rates are increasing.

A bride is unveiled in a traditional Mongolian wedding.

HEALTH CARE

Mongolians in the past relied on traditional Tibetan and Mongolian medicine and treatments based on local folk beliefs. Modern medical services are now provided by clinics and hospitals. Teaching preventive health care to the people was one of the priorities of the revolutionary government. Infectious diseases, such as smallpox, plague, poliomyelitis, and diphtheria, were a major problem caused by poor health habits, infrequent baths, and the difficulty of getting clean drinking water. Great effort has been put into health education, teaching the people better hygiene and how to look after babies and the elderly. Today, the average Mongolian has a life expectancy of 67.7, and infant mortality has dropped to 40 per 1,000 live births (the United States rate was 6.26 per 1,000 live births in 2000).

While modern medicine has found its place in Mongolia, traditional medicine has been retained. The Institute of Traditional Medicine in Ulaanbaatar does extensive research on folk medicine practices. It studies the ancient prescriptions and traditional methods of treatment. Special formulas use local medicinal herbs and animal parts such as antelope horns and reindeer antlers. A wolf's intestines are thought to be good for indigestion, and a woodchuck's gallbladder is believed to cure toothache and stomach complaints. Many animals are therefore hunted for their body parts as well as meat, although there are laws restricting the hunting of rare animals such as the Gobi bear, snow leopard, wild ass, and red wolf.

Over 400 kinds of plants have been found to have medicinal uses. The Institute has an outpatient center for acupuncture, massage, mineral water baths, and mud baths.

A traditional Chinese medicine practitioner weighs and prepares herbal remedies for his patients.

Promising young
Mongolian students
used to be sent by
the state to the
Soviet Union for
higher education.
Many still pursue
advanced studies
abroad. Russia and
Germany are favored
destinations.

HIGH LITERACY RATE

In prerevolutionary days, religion and education were interlinked. There was no secular education. Monasteries took on the task of teaching children Tibetan and how to chant and pray. In higher classes in the monasteries, the older and more privileged children who proved themselves up to the effort were taught subjects such as philosophy, art, astrology, and medicine. But the large majority, the children of herders, received no formal education at all.

Following the revolution, the government sought to eradicate illiteracy among both children and adults. The first primary (elementary) school was set up just a month after the government came to power. Primary schools were promptly built. Boarding schools allowed the children of nomadic families to live comfortably away from home during the school term. The government also started a drive to educate adults. Teachers were sent to homes to teach short-term courses in the evenings. Everyone who could read and write was given the obligation of teaching those who could not. The international agency UNESCO has awarded the N. K. Krupskaya Medal to the Mongolian Institute of Language and Literature of the Academy of Sciences

Students in a classroom in Mongolia.

to acknowledge the literacy program's success. It is estimated that more than 97.8 percent of Mongolians are now literate.

Education is free and compulsory for all children from 6 to 14. Children from the age of 3 may attend kindergarten and learn the basics of reading, writing, and counting. Students aged 6 to 18 years attend either secondary schools for university preparation or vocational and technical schools, learning skills in areas such as construction, manufacturing, transportation, communication, and agriculture that will enable them in time to join the workforce. Since 2008 there has been a transition from an 11- to a 12-year schooling system, though a full cycle is rarely completed by rural adolescents.

In 1922 the first special secondary school was set up to train teachers. There are now 18 such schools providing training in more than 100 fields, including education, law, and medicine.

Mongolia's State University was opened in 1942. Some departments, such as the Agricultural Institute, Medical Institute, and Russian Language Pedagogical Institute, have become separate institutions. There are nine universities, and over four dozen secondary, technical, and vocational schools, as well as a number of private schools and colleges.

A statue of Horloogiyn Choybalsan, a communist-era leader, stands in front of the National University of Mongolia in Ulaanbaatar.

RELIGION

Serene Buddha images in the Erdene Zuu monastery in Karakorum.

CHAPTER 8

ABOUT HALF OF ALL Mongolians are Buddhists. There are also Muslims and Christians, though the traditional and most ancient religion in the country is shamanism, which is based on the belief that the spirit world is present in nature. It survives still in Mongolia, though it is not as prevalent as it was not long ago.

Mongolians are by law free to follow any religion they choose. The constitution guarantees freedom of worship, a legacy handed down from the time of Genghis Khan, when the ancient capital of Karakorum was a place where many religions, including shamanism, Christianity, Islam, Confucianism, Taoism, and Buddhism were practiced side by side.

An intricately decorated temple in Mongolia.

The link between Mongolia and Tibet is very strong. Every Mongolian Buddhist hopes to make a pilgrimage to the holy city of Lhasa, Tibet, at least once in his lifetime.

Mongolians, like
Tibetans, gain
spiritual merit by
turning prayer
wheels, which are
hollow cylinders
filled with
thousands of small
paper prayer slips.
Each revolution of
the wheel adds
to the believer's
merit savings
account.

BUDDHISM

Buddhism came to Mongolia very early from the Uighur people, who belong to one of the most advanced civilizations in Central Asia.

Although shamanism was the most influential religion then, the aristocracy, including Genghis himself, was sympathetic to Buddhism. It was only in the 13th century that Buddhism gained real influence. A Tibetan monk who was known by the title of Phagspa Lama became the spiritual head of the country and granted special status to all Buddhist priests, called lamas. They were exempted from military duty and taxes. Buddhism was not widespread, however, because it was the religion of the ruling classes. With the collapse of Kublai Khan's Yuan dynasty, Buddhism lost its influence in Mongolia.

Not until the 16th century did Buddhism again become widespread. Mongolian society was in a bad state. Many Mongol leaders were fighting among themselves for power, and people were unhappy and in despair. The rulers felt that a strong religion, such as Buddhism, would strengthen their leadership roles and provide the people with moral fiber. At that time, there was an ongoing rivalry between the Red Hat and Yellow Hat sects of Tibetan Buddhism; each side hoped to gain power through the support of the Mongols. The Chinese Ming dynasty was also anxious to have the Mongols embrace religion, hoping that Buddhism would pacify the restless and warlike Mongols.

In 1578 the Mongol ruler Altan Khan invited the Tibetan religious head, Sonam Gyatsho, to Mongolia and gave him the title of Dalai Lama. In return, Altan obtained recognition as the reincarnation of Kublai Khan. These grand gestures reestablished the spiritual links between Mongolia and Tibet. Shamanism and all its practices were effectively banned. The lamas hurriedly adapted shamanist rituals to Buddhist rites to ease the spread of Buddhism.

From then on, Buddhism grew in influence. Translations of large numbers of Buddhist sacred texts from Tibetan into Mongolian helped to make Buddhism accessible to the people. Monasteries were built all over the country and gained in popularity and influence, mainly because the chief priests were often local princes and other people with wide authority in society. Many lamas were philosophers, scientists, historians, artists, and craftspeople, and the monasteries became centers of learning, influential cultural oases.

Gombordorji Zanabazar, the Jebtsundamba, was a famous reincarnate lama and head of Buddhism in Mongolia. He built the Ih Hüree monastery in Urga in 1651 and many others. He translated many Buddhist texts. He was also a consummate sculptor and painter of religious statues and scrolls. Seven other Jebtsundamba rulers followed him, but all of them were from Tibet because the Chinese Qing emperors were afraid a Mongol might stir up political trouble. The eighth Jebtsundamba did just that, declaring Mongolia independent of Chinese rule. When he died in 1924, the communist government stopped the search for a successor.

Religious persecution began in 1932. In 1937, under Choibalsan, a former lama who turned revolutionary, more than 17,000 monks vanished in purges. Of more than 700 monasteries, only 4 were left standing to serve as museums of the "feudal period." Religious ceremonies were outlawed except at Gandantegchinlin monastery (also called Gandan) in Ulaanbaatar until 1990. Religious practices were allowed once again in the 1990s.

MONASTERIES

In the early 1990s the decline of communist rule led to the rehabilitation of religion. About 2,000 lamas established small communities at the sites of some 120 former monasteries, and many monasteries that were damaged during the persecution of the 1930s were restored.

Lamas chant, ring bells, blow horns, and beat drums during prayers at Gandan monastery.

Reincarnation is a basic Buddhist belief. Reincarnate lamas are identified by interpreting omens and dreams, and a potential lama is tested. Zanabazar was said to be able to recite Tibetan texts at the age of five, without ever having learned this language.

The three big monasteries in Mongolia are the Gandan monastery in Ulaanbaatar, the Erdene Zuu in Karakorum, and the Amarba-yasgalant monastery near Darkhan. Gandan, the largest and most important center of Buddhism, was built in 1838. Its library houses thousands of rare books and manuscripts in Tibetan, Mongolian, and other languages. The monastery is the headquarters of the Asian Buddhist Conference for Peace, an organization made up of members from many Asian countries.

SHAMANISM

Shamanism, characterized by supernatural insights of a shaman, or priest, was very important in the spiritual life of the people until the 16th century. During the rule of Genghis Khan its practice played a big role. The people believed that Genghis received his authority to rule from Tengri, the supreme sky god. There were many shamans in Genghis's court who acted as intermediaries between the people and the unseen spirit world. A chief

The Erdene Zuu monastery in Karakorum is probably the oldest in Mongolia.

shaman could determine, with the help of his bond to the spirit world, when it was time to break camp, where the khan's camp should go next, and when it was the right time to go to war. The shaman could make countless other big and small decisions. The shaman helped to cure illnesses, drive away evil spirits, find lost animals, and make predictions, and was consulted for a favorable date on which to hold an important event such as cutting a child's hair for the first time, doing business, or getting married.

Mongolia shares a tradition of shamanism with many other hunting-gathering cultures in Central Asia and North America. A shaman most often comes from a family with a tradition of shamanism. Both men and women can be shamans.

A person destined to become a shaman is usually identified by some uncommon behavior such as fainting spells or visions. The candidate takes years to learn to communicate with the spirits. The process includes prolonged fasts, living like a hermit, and interpreting dreams and visions, his own and others'.

FOLK BELIEFS

A typical shaman found in Mongolia, dressed for intervention.

Many myths and beliefs connected with shamanism explain the relationship between the heavens and the people, the creation of the world, and the role of nature. It is believed that there are three worlds: the heavenly upper world ruled by Tengri, the earthly middle world inhabited by people, and the subterranean lower world, ruled over by Erleg Khan (ER-leg khan), where the souls of the dead await reincarnation. The sky is male, and the earth is female.

Many folk beliefs are connected with the countryside, and these are based on a belief in the sacredness of mountains, lakes, and other natural objects. Mongolians are superstitious, believing in charms, strange events, and miracles. Everyday objects may possess magical qualities. For example,

An ovoo (AW-waw) is a shrine on a mountain slope or near a lake or river in the countryside that often looks like a pile of stones or rocks placed in a pyramidal shape. Bottles of vodka, a bit of tobacco, some colored scraps of cloth, even some money or candy are often placed on the ovoo as an offering to the gods. When a person comes across an ovoo, he usually walks around it three times in a clockwise direction and adds some kind of offering to the collection already there.

Every so often a small religious ceremony is held at the site of an ovoo. Lamas say prayers accompanied by libations, or the pouring of liquor, usually airag, on the shrine, and people make offerings. There is usually some feasting followed by a minifestival of sports. This ritual usually celebrates the coming of spring. It is also held to pray for good weather, abundant rainfall, plentiful grass for the animals, and successful hunting.

This ceremony, which once was prohibited, has made a comeback with the greater freedom of democracy in the 1990s.

the stirrup is important in a horse-riding society, and when a man leaves on a long trip, milk is sprinkled on it to bless it. Many superstitions concern animals. Because the peacock is sacred, Mongolian homes often display peacock feathers to purify the room. Crows and snakes are believed to cast spells, and a goose is considered capable of breaking a stirrup if the rider does something bad to the bird. It is believed that one's very own star shines when one is born and disappears from the sky when one dies. If one is very lucky or has a happy life, it is due to one's lucky star.

ISLAM AND CHRISTIANITY

Muslims make up about 6 percent of the total population. Most are Kazakhs living in Bayan-Ölgi in the west. The Muslims also suffered during the persecution of religion under the communists, when many mosques were closed or destroyed, just as the Buddhist monasteries were. Some have been reopened or are being rebuilt.

Christians form less than 4 percent of the population. A law passed in 1993 regarding state and church relations restricted religious activities largely in favor of Buddhism. This law made it difficult for Christian churches to organize themselves, though many of the laws have been repealed or relaxed after constitutional challenges in court.

Sunday Mass at the Roman Catholic Peter and Paul Cathedral in Ulaanbaatar.

Mongolian posters in Ulaanbaatar.

CHAPTER 9

THE MONGOLIAN LANGUAGE, like its culture, has been shaped by the many historical influences that have impacted the country and its people over the centuries. This is especially evident in the written form of the language.

SPOKEN LANGUAGE

Mongolian is spoken by most of the people of Mongolia and also by those living in Inner Mongolia, which is part of China. It is also spoken by groups of people living in other provinces of China and in the Russian Federation.

A young vendor amid the display in a Mongolia bookshop.

The written Mongolian of today dates back to the 13th century. It has survived many changes over time, and like all languages, it has kept the elements that work best.

Mongolian is part of the Altaic family of languages that is spoken over a wide area from Turkey in the west to the Pacific Ocean in the east. Many different dialects are spoken by the various Mongolian tribes, but there are basically four main ones.

Khalkha is the dialect spoken by most Mongolians and on which the official language is based. The other three main ones are the Western or Oirat dialects, spoken in the western parts of the country; the Buriad dialect, spoken in the north around Lake Baikal; and the Inner Mongolian dialects of the south.

Many Mongolians, having been educated in Russia, are also fluent in Russian. English is becoming a popular second language.

WRITING IT DOWN

When writing became necessary for administrative and religious missionary work, the Mongols developed their written script by borrowing characters from other people. Their script has changed many times.

The written language in use today dates back to the 13th century. According to Mongolian history, Genghis Khan decreed that there be devised a proper written Mongolian language. After conquering the Uighur people, he commanded his captive Uighur adviser, Tatatungo, to adapt the ancient Uighur Script to the Mongolian language. The long, stringlike letters were connected by continuous lines from top to bottom and read from left to right.

An example of classical Mongolian script. The earliest Mongolian writing, the Stone of Chinggis, is a 13-century inscription of the archery feats of Yisüngge, Chinggis's nephew.

When Kublai Khan was in power, he wanted a new written language to unite the many different languages of his far-flung empire. He ordered the Tibetan scholar and monk Phagspa Lama to devise a new alphabet. The Square Script, with square-shaped letters, emerged for a short period of time. It was based on the Tibetan and Indian alphabets and was written from top to bottom. It was the official script of the Yuan dynasty. When Kublai's rule ended, the script fell into disuse, although examples remain in inscriptions in temples, seals, and title pages of ancient books.

In the 17th century two other handwritings were invented. Both the Clear Script, which tried to bring the written language closer to the spoken language, and the Horizontal Square Script, based on an ancient form of Indian writing, could transcribe and record words in Mongolian, Tibetan, and Sanskrit.

In the early 20th century yet one more, the Vaghintara Script, was invented for transcribing Russian words into Mongolian. All three scripts were short-lived.

A student learning to read Mongolian, using headphones.

The Soyombo (SOH-yom-bo) script was introduced by Gombordorji Zanabazar in 1686. It was such a complex and ornamental script that it became impractical for wide use. Instead, it was limited to religious applications in prayers and religious texts. What has remained of this script, however, is the Soyombo symbol, which has been adopted as the Mongolian national emblem of freedom and independence. It is depicted in the state emblem and in the national flag.

At the very top of the Soyombo symbol is a flame symbolizing blossoming, revival, and the continuation of the family. The three points of the flame symbolize the past, present, and future prosperity of the people. Below the flame is the sun and the crescent moon, symbolizing the origin of the Mongolian people. The flame, sun, and moon together express the determination that the Mongolian people may always live and prosper.

Next come some geometric forms—triangles and rectangles. The triangles express the wish for freedom and independence, while the horizontal rectangles at the sides symbolize honesty, justice, and nobility. The broader, vertical rectangles symbolize the walls of a fortress. In the middle of the geometric section of the emblem are two intertwined fish, which resemble the Chinese yin-yang symbol and signify natural complements like male and female or night and day. In Mongolian folklore, fish never close their eyes and are therefore vigilant creatures. This part of the Soyombo emblem expresses the belief that the Mongolian people will stay united so that they are stronger than the walls of a fortress.

While Mongolia was under Soviet influence, the Mongolian script was replaced by Cyrillic, an alphabet that was developed in the ninth century based on Greek characters and was the foundation of the Russian script. Cyrillic writing cannot represent some of the sounds in spoken Mongolian. Still, the Mongolian written language today is based on Cyrillic, with some modifications. The alphabet has 26 letters, and it is written from the top down, left to right. Since Mongolia's declaring its independence from Soviet influence, there arose popular interest in reviving the traditional script of Genghis Kahn. In 1990 the government resolved to reintroduce the Mongolian script by 1994, but this plan has yet to be implemented.

MEDIA

The beginnings of Mongolian language newspapers date to the end of the 19th century and early 20th century when both the Soviet Union and China became more interested in increasing their influence in Mongolia. A Mongolian newspaper was published in the early 1900s by the Mongolian

There is a great variety of words for grasses and animals and many variations of such words. *Mori* is a gelding. *Xiimori* is a flying magic horse, and the word also means "healthy." *Morisaitai* means "fortunate," or a person who owns a good horse. The *morin khuur* is a traditional horse-head fiddle.

A family inside a *ger*. Television watching is a popular pastime.

A man reading a local newspaper, one of hundreds published throughout the nation.

literati who wanted to liberate their country from Chinese rule. To counter the influence of the paper, China-inspired journals in Mongolian were distributed in Mongolia but found few readers. During the revolution, Mongolian revolutionaries published their own paper, the *Mongolian Truth* (*Mongolyn Ünen*), which became the voice of the Mongolian People's Revolutionary Party. Now known as *Ünen* (*Truth*), it is the most widely read paper in the nation, with about 200,000 subscribers. There are more than 20 national newspapers.

With greater freedom and democracy, there now are hundreds of small newspapers and other publications. Papers and journals produced by trade unions, the army, and scientific, literary, artistic, and cultural organizations have proliferated also.

The Mongolian state-run radio made its first broadcast in 1931. It broadcasts government programs as well as traditional folk music, epics, and Western classical music. Another station caters to young people, playing modern Western pop, often with English-speaking deejays. Radio Ulaanbaatar, a privately owned station, offers even more English-speaking programs and Western music. The radio is a very important source of information and entertainment, especially in rural areas. A portable radio is the herder's inseparable companion.

The programs on Ulaanbaatar television, which started broadcasting in 1967, and other stations are largely Russian movies dubbed in Mongolian, and locally produced documentaries, newscasts, and sports programs, especially wrestling, which is extremely popular. National television programs are beamed to all the *aimag* capitals and to more than 50 other administrative centers. In 2008, there were approximately 68 broadcast stations.

MONGOLIAN NAMES

Mongolian names usually consist of two names. The first is the patronymic name, or the father's name, often in a possessive form; the second is the given name. So, former prime minister Yumjaagiyn Tsedenbal's given name is Tsedenbal. His father is Yumjaag. People are usually called by their given name. The patronymic name is always used with the given name, but is rarely used in speech. When there is a title indicating a person's rank or age, it comes after the name. For example, Mr. Tsedenbal is Tsedenbal *guai* (GOO-ai).

NONVERBAL LANGUAGE

Mongolians use the right hand to gesture with and to take things. When receiving a gift, food, or snuff, it is proper to do it with both hands; the right hand only may be used but with the left hand touching the right elbow as if in support. Mongolians beckon someone with the fingers of the right hand, a little outstretched, palm facing down.

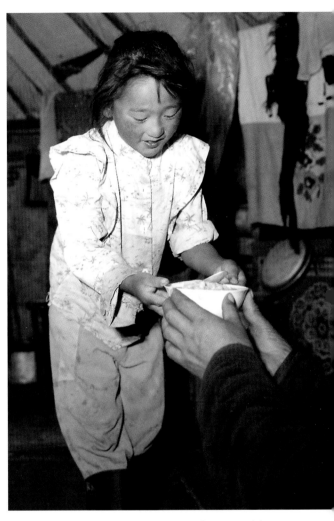

A young girl politely offering tea to an elder, with both hands holding the bowl.

In the city a handshake is acceptable. In a traditional greeting between two people of different age or status, the one younger or lower in status gently supports the forearms of the other. This greeting is also used to show respect to elders during the Lunar New Year. It is impolite to point with one finger; all the fingers are used. Other taboos are crossing one's legs and kicking someone, even accidentally. An immediate apology is due. It is rude to stare directly into the eyes of an elder. Women cover their mouths in a gesture of modesty when laughing.

In greetings, an inquiry about health is added as well as a question concerning a seasonal activity, for example, "How was the harvest?"

ARTS

A stunning coral mask representing
Begze, the god of war.

A N OBSERVER MIGHT EXPECT Mongolian society to be rather underdeveloped from a cultural and artistic point of view, as it is basically a nomadic society with people remaining hardly long enough in any place to build lasting monuments or buildings.

Mongolians, however, though still largely nomadic, do have a deep cultural heritage going back many thousands of years. They expressed their artistic creativity in everyday articles, such as saddles and boots and hunting tools, which they lovingly made and decorated.

A crafted Mongolian saddle with decorated stirrup straps and pommel.

Two significant 19th-century Mongolian writers were Noyon hutagt Ravjaa and B. Inji-nash. Noyon hutagt Ravjaa wrote many religious treatises, but his popularity lives in the more than 400 nonreligious poems and songs he composed, including "Fair Wind," "The Charming," and "The Four Seasons of the Year." B. Injinash's most famous work was the *Köke Sudur*, or "Blue Chronicle," a fictional version of Mongol history extolling humanistic and patriotic ideals.

This stark carving of a stone man was discovered in the desolate Mongolian landscape.

Before writing was invented, there was a very strong oral tradition that recalled history through the telling of epic stories, folktales, and songs. Itinerant singers and storytellers traveled across mountains and steppes, performing in return for food, shelter, and money.

Later, Mongolian art and architecture served religion, as statues and paintings were created, and monasteries and temples were built and embellished by skilled artisans.

BRONZE AGE CULTURE

Mongolia is said to have been inhabited from very early times, and many scholars believe that humans from this part of Central Asia migrated north, crossed the land bridge, and populated North America—the earliest stock of the first Americans! Stone tools dating back some 500,000 years have been found in Mongolia. The oldest evidence of some sort of art and culture comes from the Bronze Age, which goes back to approximately 3000 B.C. or earlier in Mongolia.

The people, though nomadic, carved and shaped retangular stone monuments called "reindeer stones" and placed them upright in valleys, open grasslands, and hillsides, probably as markers of sacred sites or graves; these were possibly the beginnings of *ovoo*, or shaman shrines. The stones are from 3 to 13 feet (1 to 4 m) high and bear images of celestial bodies such as the sun or the moon in the upper section, graceful running and jumping deer in the middle section, and images of tools and weapons, including knives, swords, hooks, bows and quivers of arrows, and axes in the bottom section.

The artists of the sixth to eighth centuries had greater carving ability. They created lifelike statues of people complete with clothing of that period and the weapons and tools they used. This representational tradition continued into the 13th century.

PAINTING AND SCULPTURE

Painting in Mongolia dates back to the eighth century with the paintings of the Uighur. Later painting took on a religious significance and had Buddhist themes. The paintings were done on cloth, using mineral and vegetable dyes, and were often framed with silk. Traditionally they had red, white, or black backgrounds. Some religious "paintings" were appliqués created by sewing pieces of silk and other fabrics onto larger pieces of cloth. These silk paintings decorated many temples and palaces. Religious paintings hang in many homes today.

Intricate and colorful paintings of deities cover the main door of the Bogo Khan Palace.

Hamilton East Public Library

Mongolian painting next took on a form called Mongol *zurag* (ZOO-rug), which is distinctive in almost completely filling the space, the use of certain colors, and a two-dimensional, flat style. These depict the simple life and traditions of the people. The best-known painter of this school is Balduugiyn Sharav (1869—1920s). His most famous work is *One Day in the Life of Mongolia*. Landscape artist L. Gavaa and portrait painters O. Tsevegjav (1915—75) and U. Yadamsüren (1905—86) further developed the style of Mongol *zurag*.

Sculpture had religious themes. Zanabazar (1635—1723), Mongolia's most famous sculptor and painter, created many religious statues and paintings. He learned bronze casting from the Tibetans, and his works include bronze statues of Buddhist deities, especially Tara, the deity of compassion.

LITERATURE

Mongolian heroic epics—tales of war and empire, myths of origin, histories of the Great Khans—were written down more than 750 years ago. The earliest and most

A bronze casting of a bodhisattva by Zanabazar (1635-1723), the first Jebtsundamba Khutuktu, the spiritual head of Buddhism in Mongolia. He was also a renowned painter.

important story ever written is *The Secret History of the Mongols*, about the origin of the greatest Mongol ever, Genghis Khan.

After the decline of the Mongol Empire, the tradition of storytelling continued into the 15th and 16th centuries, with stories about the power struggles among the many tribal princes.

The 17th century saw the rise of philosophical and didactic poetry by the lamas; this coincided with the prominence of Buddhism and continued until the 19th century. Chinese poetry and stories were translated during the period spanning the 17th to the 19th centuries, including Chinese classics such as *Dream of the Red Chamber*, *Romance of the Three Kingdoms*, and *The Water Margin*.

SECRET HISTORY

The Secret History of the Mongols *describes the origin of the Mongols, particularly the birth and rise of Genghis Khan, the first ruler of Mongolia to unite the nomadic tribes of Central Asia. It is told in more than 30 stories and over 200 poems and songs. Also known as* The Sacred History of the Mongols, *it is part fact, part fable. A sample is given here.*

In the beginning Blue-gray Wolf and Beautiful Doe came from across the sea and settled at the source of the Onon River in northeast Mongolia, near Burkhan Khaldun, the "Mountain of the Shaman Spirit." Beautiful Doe gave birth to a son, Batachikhan, whose descendants pastured herds and hunted game on the slopes of the mountain.

In the 21st generation a boy was born with a clot of blood in his right fist. He was the future Chinggis (Genghis) Khan. His father, Yesugei the Brave, was the chief of

one of the Mongol tribes. At that time, there was much feuding and rivalry among the many tribes. One day, while hunting, Yesugei met a woman and her husband from another tribe and abducted her, making her his wife. Ho'elun bore him five children—four sons and a daughter. The eldest was Temüjin, "blacksmith."

Temüjin, at the age of 9, lost his father who was poisoned by a rival tribe, the Tatars. The family then lived on the banks of the river. The other tribes captured Temüjin, afraid that he would become a leader when he came of age. They made him wear a heavy wooden yoke around his neck.

Eventually Temüjin escaped, and he and his family lived like outlaws on Burkhan Khaldun. He gathered followers and grew in power. In 1206, at a great assembly of all the Mongol tribes, when he was about 40 years old, Temüjin was proclaimed Chinggis Khan—"strong ruler."

The art of reciting an epic poem is very exacting, requiring great concentration, an excellent memory, and acting and oratorical skills. Often hundreds and thousands of verses have to be learned to recite just one poem. The tradition of reciting epic poems dates back to the days when the Mongols were merely a collection of tribes, and storytellers reciting tribal history were welcomed performers. One of the most ancient epics is the story of Hüüheldei Mergen Khan, a great hunter who shoots a magic deer. Another is the story of the hero Geser, sent to earth to combat evil.

Modern Mongol literature emerged during the revolution as writers became exposed to Western and world literature, in tandem with Oriental literature, and drew inspiration from both sources. Revolutionary and nationalistic feelings were common themes of their poems, novels, and plays. Writers also translated world literature, making it possible for the people to read Lu Xun, William Shakespeare, Leo Tolstoy, Alexandre Dumas, and Rabindranath Tagore in the Mongolian language. Modern Mongolian writers of importance are Dashdorjiin Natsagdorj (1906—37), often described as the father of contemporary Mongolian literature, S. Buyannemeh (1901—37), Tsend Damdinsüren (1908—86), Donrov Namdag (1911—82), and Z. Battulag (1919—83).

ARCHITECTURE

Although nomadic, the Mongols built towns and villages; there is archaeological evidence of more than 200 ancient towns in Mongolia. These were a combination of movable homes and settlements and more permanent structures.

The intricately carved and painted ceiling of a recently restored monastery.

Karakorum, first settled by Genghis in 1220, was built by Genghis's son Ogodei in 1234 on an old Uighur site on the banks of the Orhon River. Construction was not completed until 1235, during Ogodei's rule. The city was divided into sectors for administrators, traders, craftsmen, artisans, and private individuals. The palace's main hall had a green enamel brick floor, and the roof tiles were green and red enamel. Around the palace were the residences of the princes and courtiers. Karakorum was destroyed by a Ming invasion in 1388, and today only one of the original four statuary turtles believed to protect the city from floods stands, a lonely sentinel.

Traditional flint for firemaking decorated with silver.

There were many temples and monasteries when Mongolia was the center of the Buddhist world and these were influenced by both the East and the West. The famed Erdene Zuu monastery, built in 1586, was constructed on a square plan. A brick wall topped with 108 stupas, or pagodas, spaced evenly apart, enclosed it. The huge Buddhist complex included 60 temples and housed 10,000 resident lamas.

DECORATIVE ARTS

In modern times, everyday objects and work tools are embellished with silver, embroidery, carvings, and appliqué work. Saddles, stirrups, and tools associated with horses are often carefully crafted, beautiful works of art. Intricate designs are carved on furniture, *ger* doors, hunting weapons, work tools, and musical instruments.

There are lavishly designed gold and silver accessories and wonderfully embroidered pouches and cases for carrying snuff bottles, pipes, and eating sets. Traditional clothing is also enriched with finely worked gold and silver jewelry.

A traditional Mongolian dance performed in Ulaanbaatar.

SONG AND DANCE

Mongolians love music and have developed distinctive styles. There are two basic kinds of songs, the short and the long. Short songs are usually lively and tell of everyday activities, love, and nature. Long songs are more philosophical, dealing with love, the meaning of life, and the relationship between people and nature. Long songs are formal and often performed at important functions, festivities, and ceremonies. They are harder to sing, and some songs have as many as 20,000 lines.

A special way of singing—that is not really singing but actually using the throat, tongue, mouth, and nose in a combined way to sound like a musical instrument—is called *khoomi* (KHAW-me). Professional *khoomi* singers come from certain regions where there is a strong tradition of this music. The Chandmani district of Hovd *aimag* in western Mongolia is the home of *khoomi*. Throat singing produces many different sounds by forcing air through the mouth and throat and by using the tongue to form a resonant chamber in the mouth. *Khoomi* is a tradition shared with the neighboring Tuva republic, where it is known as *khoomei*. Many other people have an interest in throat singing. Among them are Australians, Japanese, Americans, Canadians, Finns, and Irish.

Among the musical folk instruments are the *morin khuur* (MAW-rin kher), a two-stringed fiddle with a head shaped like a horse's head. The bow and strings are made from the hair of a horse's tail. It creates a beautiful yet mournful sound that comes closest to expressing the deep feelings of the heart. This instrument often accompanies the long loving songs describing the beauty of the Mongolian countryside.

Some other instruments are the *shudrag* (SHOOD-rug), a three-stringed lute with a long neck and a round wooden sound box covered with skin; the *limbe* (LIM-beh), a flute made of a simple, straight bamboo tube with at least eight finger holes; the *yoching* (YAW-ching), a board zither with two rows of 14 metal pieces stretched over a board and struck with two hammers; and the *yatag* (YAH-tug), a stringed instrument with 10 to 14 strings stretched across a long sound box.

Mongolian theater, opera, and ballet have all been influenced by the Russian forms of these arts. Russian operas are popular, but there are also Mongolian operas. The first known Mongolian opera was written by Dashdorjiin Natsagdorj. Performers were mostly trained in the Soviet Union.

Folk dancing can be seen during celebrations. The most famous dance is the Bielgee (BEE-el-gee) or Dance of the Body, typically performed by a slender girl to music. The dance usually consists of head and hand movements alone, since this dance was originally performed in *gers* where there was little space.

A group of musicians at a concert using many folk instruments.

LEISURE

Locals in an archery competition.

ongolians have always sought their leisure in much the same way as they live—by being in the countryside, close to their horses and other animals, and hunting. Their most important and traditional leisure activities are wrestling, archery, and horse racing. These friendly competitions are closely linked with the pride they feel about their history as a great and strong nation.

"The Mongol, above all things, is not a farmer. . . . On the ground, he is as awkward as a duck out of water. . . . The back of a pony is his real home. . . . He will do wonderfully well any work which keeps him in the saddle."
–Roy Chapman Andrews in *Across Mongolian Plains*

Wrestlers getting ready for a match, one of the "manly" sports in Mongolia.

Children gathered under paintings of sports in Mongolia. Horse riding and archery are two of the three "manly" sports found there.

Mongolians ride horses standing nearly upright in short stirrups. An *urgha* (OOR-ga), a willow or bamboo pole about 30 feet (9 m) long with a rope attached to the tip, is used to lasso animals.

THREE "MANLY" SPORTS

Horse racing, wrestling, and archery are known as the three "manly" sports in Mongolia, although girls and women take part in both horse racing and archery. Practically the entire country turns out to watch competitions in these three sports during the national Naadam festival that takes place each year in July.

Riding skill is necessary in a pastoral and nomadic society, with families moving with the seasons. Mongolians do not learn riding for sport but as a necessary life skill. Children learn to ride a horse almost as soon as they start walking. Practically every Mongolian knows how to ride, and they are known as excellent equestrians.

Mongolian boys are also taught to wrestle from an early age. The most promising ones are trained in special camps. They learn all the classic moves and throws, the correct wrestler's stance (supposed to be a combination of the posture of a lion and the outspread wings of a bird in flight), and the victorious "eagle dance."

Archery, the third manly sport, is practiced by men and women alike, using the same type of equipment and technique. The Mongolian bow is double-curved, made of horn, sinew, bark, and wood. Arrowheads are made of bone. The string is drawn back with the aid of a thumb ring made of leather.

TRADITIONAL GAMES

The game of "shooting bones" has been around since the time of Genghis Khan. There are several variations, but all are played with the anklebones of a lamb. Each side of the bone is shaped differently and has a name—horse, camel, goat, or sheep. A favorite form of the game uses sets of 8 or 12 bones that are "shot" at a target, two at a time, with the aid of a special wooden paddle. The winner is the player with the greatest number of bones at the end of the game.

"Catching horses" is another popular pastime among Mongolians. In this game boys in one group separate a wild horse from the rest of the herd and then chase it back at high speed. Another group of boys waits for the horse to gallop by and tries to lasso it. This exciting game develops very important skills among Mongolian boys.

HUNTING

Mongolians love hunting, which for them has a practical purpose. They shoot various animals such as deer, rabbits, and marmots for their meat, pelts, and other valuable parts. They also kill other animals that prey on livestock. Hunting used to be carried out with spears or bows and arrows. Today traps and guns have largely taken their place.

Wolves are a favorite target because they attack livestock; their pelts bring a good price, and their intestines are valued for their medicinal attributions. Marmots are also common prey almost everywhere on the steppes.

A Kazakh hunter with his farsighted hunting eagle.

Mongolian herders allow their horses to roam freely, keeping them semi-wild. They have to corral, lasso, and break in the horses again and again to use them.

Locals enjoy shopping for modern goods in the cities of Mongolia.

LEISURE IN THE CITY

Going to the movies is becoming increasingly popular, particularly among the young. Most of the films used to be from the Soviet Union and East European countries, but Hollywood films have taken an increasing hold on Mongolian moviegoers. American Westerns are very popular in Mongolia, possibly because of the scenes of wide-open spaces and cowboys on horses. Mongolians turn to television and radio to occupy much of their leisure time, especially during the winter.

Young Mongolians love listening to Western popular music, including jazz and rock. There are also a number of homegrown Mongolian rock and even heavy metal groups.

Window-shopping is an increasing leisure activity in the towns, as people enjoy looking at the varied merchandise, such as Western-style clothing.

There are many recreational spas at hot water springs that are believed to have curative effects. The government has built holiday camps for workers to go to on vacations.

MONGOLIAN CHESS

The game of chess is a very old and traditional pastime in Mongolia and is extremely popular, as also is checkers. Mongolian chess is played on a chessboard similar to the Western chessboard, but the game pieces are different, reflecting Mongolia's pastoral and nomadic lifestyle. The king, pawn, knight, castle, bishop, and queen are replaced by the khan, boy, horse, cart, camel, and lion or dog.

Naturally, the outdoors is very important even for those who live in cities, who greatly enjoy going to the countryside to visit friends and relatives. Those who can afford it retreat with their families to country *gers* or small cabins in the summer.

MODERN SPORTS

Mongolians are very sports oriented because of their nomadic traditions that keep them outdoors and physically active. The most popular games are basketball, volleyball, soccer, and gymnastics. Ulaanbaatar has a soccer stadium and an indoor coliseum. Motorcycle racing, bicycling, hang gliding, and mountain climbing draw many enthusiasts. Skiing and ice-skating on frozen rivers and lakes are extremely popular winter sports.

Sports are nurtured in schools as an important part of the curriculum. This importance is reflected in the National Games, a nationwide competition of 17 winter and summer sports organized by the country's sports clubs and associations.

Mongolians have also done well in international competitions. Their athletes take part in the Asian Games, the Olympic Games, and various world championships. They have done very well in freestyle wrestling, winning five silvers and three bronzes in the Olympic Games in the 20-year period from

There is a small film industry in Mongolia. One popular film, actually set and filmed in Inner Mongolia, is called *Urgha*. It takes a funny and humanistic look at Mongolian life and the conflict of cultures.

HOW THE CAMEL LOST ITS ANTLERS AND ITS TAIL

Once upon a time, the camel had beautiful antlers on its head and a long, luxurious tail. The deer, on the other hand, had a bald head and the horse, a thin and bedraggled tail. Both the deer and the horse envied the camel for its wonderful good looks.

One day, when the camel went down to the water to drink, it met the deer. "Could I borrow your antlers for a day?" the deer asked the camel. "There is a big celebration tonight, and I am ashamed of going with my bald head." The camel, being generous, agreed, on the condition that the deer would come to the water's edge the next day and return the antlers.

As the happy deer went on its way, holding its head up high to show off the antlers it had just gained, it met the horse. "Where did you get those antlers?" asked the horse. The deer told the horse everything. The horse thought this would be an excellent chance to fool the camel and get its lovely tail. The horse ran down to the water and to its delight saw the camel still standing there. Using the same story as the deer, the horse persuaded the camel to part with its tail.

The next morning, the camel went to the water's edge again to look for the deer and the horse and get back its possessions. But of course they did not appear. To this day, when the camel has a drink, it will take a few sips, then look up and gaze out at the steppes, hoping to catch sight of the deer and the horse, but it never does.

Mongolians use the word genin *(GEN-in) to describe the camel and the same word to describe a person who is too generous for his or her own good.*

1968 to 1988. In the 2008 Summer Olympics in Beijing, Mongolia took home two gold and two silver medals.

FOLKTALES

The telling of folktales is an old and important tradition. Besides the entertainment provided, folktales transmit traditions and values from one generation to the next. Storytellers are usually older folk, but there are also professional storytellers who tell stories for money, food, and shelter, often accompanying their stories with songs.

THE MONGOLIAN CIRCUS

Although it emerged only in the 1930s, the circus is now a unique form of art in Mongolia and a direct result of Soviet influence. Following a tour by a Soviet circus troupe in 1931, the first group of aspiring Mongolian circus artistes was sent to the Soviet Union for training.

In the 70-some years it has been in existence, the Mongolian circus has performed all over the world, and won medals in circus competitions. A specialty of the circus is contortionism, in which artistes perform complicated contorted postures, while in precarious balancing positions. This act has become a highlight of the Mongolian circus. Circus acts are sometimes performed in the open air in the countryside, even in trees.

Many folktales are about animals with human qualities as the main characters. The snake is often a bad character; so is the hedgehog, though not as bad as the snake. The lion, the dragon, the elephant, and the mythical *garuda* (ga-ROO-da)—part eagle part man, who guards a sacred mountain—are strong animals with good attributes. The horse is often magical and intelligent, capable of incredible feats, including flying. Although a man may seem to be the hero in a story, it is the horse that often steals the limelight as the real hero, giving the rider advice, warning of dangers, and foretelling the events to come. The camel is thought of as kind and generous and often too trusting of others.

Stories depicting ordinary, simple folk, with qualities such as honesty, wisdom, and kindness, who triumph over evil, greed, and injustice of all kinds include such favorite characters as the clever Badarchin, a wandering lama; the storyteller Dalan Hudalch; and the witty Tsartsan Namjil.

FESTIVALS

Masked actors bring a touch of culture into
the fun-filled festivities of Naadam.

BEFORE THE REVOLUTION, many festivals in Mongolia were connected with days of religious significance. Celebrations were also held to mark important events such as weddings. After the revolution, however, the state's efforts to stamp out religion led to most holidays becoming celebrations of socialist and state objectives such as the solidarity of workers.

Each year in the 12-year lunar cycle is named for an animal, beginning with the year of the rat, followed by those of the ox, tiger, rabbit, dragon, snake, horse, sheep or goat, monkey, cockerel, dog, and pig. Years have alternating male and female characteristics. The male (called "hard" years) are the rat, tiger, dragon, horse, monkey, and dog years. The rest are female, or "easy," years.

Soldiers taking part in the opening ceremony of the Naadam festival in Mongolia.

Only two traditional festivals, New Year's Day and Naadam, have survived. Naadam, the biggest and most popular observation of the year, has become a national holiday and is held from July 11 to 13.

There are annual events such as the Golden Autumn Music Festival and the Snowdrop Music Festival for Children. Some other festivals are produced only every five years, such as the International Circus Festival and National Amateur Folklore Art Festival.

Parties are held for special events such as the birth of a child, the erection of a new *ger*, a child's first haircut, the first day of making *airag* and new felt, and on special days for herdsmen, camel breeders, and milkmaids.

NEW YEAR'S DAY

The exact day for the start of a new year depends on the lunar calendar, but it usually falls between the end of January and early February. New Year's Day is known as "White Moon" or "White Month."

Children participating in the Children's Day celebrations in Mongolia.

A throng of spectators watching at the popular Naadam festivities.

On New Year's Eve the family gathers at the home of the oldest member for a celebratory meal. On New Year's Day, milk and *airag* are offered to the spirit of the sky, and each family member has to walk in the direction specified by a book of omens. Finally, family members greet each other with good wishes. The oldest member of the family is the first to be greeted. Once the greetings have been exchanged, the rest of the day is spent in eating, drinking, and socializing. A festive table is usually set up in each home. People go from house to house visiting family and friends.

Activities, such as horse races, wrestling, and other competitions, are organized by local community leaders as part of the New Year celebrations.

NAADAM

Naadam is the best-known festival and biggest event of the year. It marks the high point of the summer when people travel hundreds of miles across the country to various previously announced meeting grounds where they can celebrate with sports, games, and feasting. Since 1922 the biggest Naadam occurs in Ulaanbaatar to celebrate Mongolia's National Day.

For days before the big Naadam, people ride in on their horses—families in trucks and on horse-drawn wooden carts—and set up their *gers* just outside the city. The thick smell of cooking smoke hangs over the encampment. The makeshift town grows as people gather and wait for the entertainment and festivities to begin with a colorful opening ceremony featuring marchers and music in the national stadium.

Naadam is a sports-oriented festival, and the most exciting events are the contests in wrestling, archery, and horse riding. Hundreds of wrestlers come from all over the country to test their strength and skill against each other. The wrestling contests take place in the national stadium. There are no weight categories or age limits as in international wrestling competitions, but the wrestlers are all big and muscular men. Traditionally, either 512 or 1,024 wrestlers take part in the contest, which lasts throughout the two or three days of the Naadam festival.

Undaunted by her age, this five-year-old girl is taking part in the Naadam horse races.

Participants in horse riding are 5- to 12-year-old boys and girls. Races are run over courses from 10 to 20 miles (16 to 32 km). The distance is set by the horse's age, not the child's. The children often ride bareback, already being skilled riders and tacticians who have trained for the event. They know how to conserve the horse's energy to go the distance and to find that extra spurt near the finish line.

Before the race begins, the young riders pace three times around the starting point in the stadium, giving an ancient war cry. They wear bright and colorful clothes with symbols of good luck on their backs. The course itself takes them once around the stadium, then out into the country where they have to negotiate numerous obstacles such as rivers and hills.

The winning riders do laps of honor around the stadium and canter up to the grandstand to receive the ceremonial bowls of *airag*, of which they drink a little, pouring the rest on the horses. Honor is also paid to the less fortunate losers. They are led up to the grandstand together with their mounts, while the spectators shout words of encouragement and appreciation for their efforts, and a special chant is said in their honor.

Archery, though called a "manly" sport, has women participants, too. The archers are dressed in *del* and traditional pointed hats. Both men and women use the same kind of bow and shooting technique. When a target is hit, a group of judges sings out a short ceremonial song of praise. The winner of the archery contest is declared "sharpshooter."

"Sharpshooter" hopefuls participating in an archery contest during Naadam.

RELIGIOUS MASKED DANCE FESTIVAL

The religious masked dance festival called Tsam was performed in big Buddhist monasteries in ancient times. It originated in India and spread to Tibet. From there, it was taken to Mongolia in the 16th century. Part dance and part mystery play, the masked dance was based on Buddhist mythology, forming part of Buddhist rites.

The masks were made from papier-mâché and decorated with precious stones, metals, and coral. They were vividly colored in red, black, yellow, white, and blue, and were bigger than life size so they could be seen clearly and appreciated by the audience. The masks depicted Buddhist deities such as the fierce protector gods and Yama, or Tshoijoo, the Lord of Death. The Mongolian costumes, masks, and sets were different from those in Tibet.

The dances frequently described the triumph of good over evil, with characters such as the funny White Old Man, a buffoon, the Dark Old Man in his black mask and white fangs, and Garuda, the mountain god. These were elements of witchcraft and shamanism.

A performer uses the Tshoijoo mask during a Tsam Dance. Tshoijoo is believed to be the king of the underworld in Tibetan Buddhism.

Local dancers performing the uplifting Eagle Dance.

From the 16th to the 19th centuries each of the 700 major monasteries staged a big performance, called Tsam, once a year. The last Tsam was held in Ulaanbaatar in the late 1930s. After that the communist suppression of Buddhism banned such traditions. There is a reawakening of interest in the dance, with old monks teaching younger ones the steps and rituals.

HAIRCUTTING CEREMONY

The haircutting ceremony occurs when a child is 3 to 5 years old and is believed to have survived the dangers of infancy. It is an old nomadic tradition that is celebrated with great joy. Haircutting normally takes place in the fall.

Traditionally the day is chosen by a lama. Days beforehand, the preparation of celebratory dishes begins, and on the big day the festive table is laden with food and drink.

The child goes from guest to guest with a pair of scissors and a ceremonial blue silk bag. Each person cuts off a little lock of hair, puts it in the bag, and gives the child a present or gift of money. Throughout the ceremony everyone eats, drinks, and talks festively.

FOOD

This food market in Mongolia is well stocked.

MEAT (THE FATTER THE BETTER) and dairy products are Mongolians' main foods. Both are readily available from the domestic animals they raise: camels, cattle, goats, and sheep. It is unlikely to meet a Mongolian vegetarian unless he happens to be a Buddhist monk.

The short growing season makes the cultivation of vegetables quite difficult. Vegetable farming was left to the Chinese, and that was only after the 1932 revolution when the government introduced farming into the economy.

A typical Mongolian meal with its generous choices of dairy products.

"Mongolians, we quickly learned, love meat and fat, and in fact consider meat without fat unappetizing and inadequate. Once, when we were trying to buy meat, . . . a young man we knew brought us a leg of mutton but refused payment because he said the meat wasn't good quality. It was lean, and taking money would be like cheating us."
–M. C. Goldstein and C. M. Beal in *The Changing World of Mongolia's Nomads*

Fresh breads and sweet pastries are found mostly in urban bakeries.

Mongolians eat three regular meals a day. Breakfast and lunch usually consist of dairy foods and sometimes meat. Meat is typically present at the evening meal. Tea is drunk throughout the day. The whole family gathers for dinner, often eating boiled lamb, a favorite dish, and noodle soup.

The eating utensils used depends on the food. Mongolians use chopsticks for noodles, spoons for vegetables and rice, and knives for cutting meat. Hardly any seasoning except salt is used. In more recent times, there has been an increase in the availability of imported food, particularly in the capital, Ulaanbaatar. Western-style supermarkets have appeared and compete with the more traditional Mongolian market stalls. There are many restaurants, bakeries, and tea shops whose customers tend to be among the more well-to-do in local society. Mongolian, Western, and Asian cuisines can all be found in these eateries. The American hot dog is a popular alternative to the lamb sausage.

LAMB IS THE BEST

Mongolians enjoy beef and lamb, especially the latter. Very little of the sheep is wasted. Besides the meat, the lungs, heart, stomach, intestines, liver, and blood are boiled and eaten. Horsemeat is popular among the Kazakhs in the west. Besides the meat of their domestic animals, Mongolians also like eating marmots, rabbit, deer, and wild boar. Meat that cannot be used soon is dried and preserved.

Lamb is often prepared by cutting it into joints and smaller pieces, then boiled or made into a stew. *Buuz* (BUHZ), a national dish, is a dumpling filled with chopped lamb. *Khuurshuur* (KHER-sher) is a fried pancake made of flour and lamb. Sheep's blood and intestines are the chief ingredients of a sausagelike dish. Barbecued lamb is called *shorlog* (SHOR-log). *Khorkhog* (KHOR-kohg) is usually cooked on special occasions such as festivals. A goat or sheep is killed, dressed, and placed on hot coals, then hot rocks are put inside the carcass so that it is cooked evenly from the inside out.

Animal fat is relished. Chunks of fat often float in the stews. The Mongolian fat-tailed sheep, a special breed, has a tail that is usually cooked as a delicacy. It is so fatty that it weighs more than 20 pounds (9 kg).

Fresh goat meat being sold in a local market. Beef and lamb are also sold.

The quality of commonly available tea is very poor. Bits of tea leaves, twigs, and other impurities are pressed into bricks for easy storage and transportation. The tea bricks are so hard that small chunks have to be chipped off with a knife or hammer before being steeped in boiling water.

Onions, potatoes, and cabbage have crept into the diet only recently. People in the countryside, especially the less affluent, eat mainly pickled vegetables rather than fresh vegetables and fruit.

A staple food for Mongolians is a soft pastry, rolled out and formed into shapes, then deep-fried. Large amounts of this are eaten at mealtimes with meat, cheeses, and tea. Rice, noodles, and bread are also staples. Fish and chicken are not common foods in the Mongolian diet.

WHITE FOOD

Dairy products from camels, mares, sheep, goats, and cows are called "white food," second only to meat as the most important food.

Women milk the animals, then boil the milk. The skin that forms on the surface is skimmed off and dried slightly to make a soft, creamy, pancakelike food, a delicacy eaten on its own or spread on pastries. To make *arkhi* (AHR-khee), an alcoholic drink, boiled cow's milk is put into a leather bag, standard

Freshly made cheese is dried in the sun,

household equipment found in every *ger*, and left to ferment. It is stirred with a long wooden paddle every day, churning the milk into butter, which is removed and eaten. The remaining buttermilk is used for the *arkhi*. All dairy products are made in the summer and fall. Curds from coagulated milk and various cheeses are dried and keep well for months, and are thus always available for food during the winter months. Despite consuming huge quantities of dairy products and animal fat, studies have not discovered any unusually high levels of cholesterol among the population, possibly because of the heavy physical work of the nomads!

A family enjoys a typical meal consisting of meat, dumplings, and tea.

MILK TEA

Mongolians drink tea at meals and in between. There is usually a big pot of tea in the *ger* always ready. Milk tea is made by boiling tea leaves in water and adding some milk, butter, and salt gradually to the mixture. It is stirred by scooping it with a ladle and pouring it back into the pot from some height. Sometimes when milk is not available, herders make the tea with salted water, letting it boil for a while.

BUUZ AND KHUURSHUUR (LAMB DUMPLINGS)

2 servings

1 cup (250 ml) ground lamb

Pepper and salt to taste

1 cup (250 ml) flour

¼ teaspoon (1 ml) each of paprika, marjoram and/or cumin

¼ cup (60 ml) water (adding a little more if dough seems dry)

- Mix the ground lamb with pepper, salt, and one or more of the optional spices. Add a dash of salt and water, a little at a time, to the flour, kneading until the dough is firm. Roll out the dough to ⅛ of an inch (3 mm) thick. Use a cookie cutter or a glass tumbler dipped in flour to cut out circles of dough 4—6 inches (10—15 cm) in diameter.

- Put a little ground lamb in the center of each circle. Bring up the edges of the dough so that it forms a ball in your hand. Pinch the edges of the dough together, leaving a little gap open at the top.

- Place the balls in a steamer. Steam about 15—20 minutes until the meat is cooked. The *buuz* is ready to be served.

- For *khuurshuur*, use the same ingredients, but put the ground lamb in one-half of the circle and flip the other half over it. Pinch the edges together. Deep-fry the pastry in hot oil until light brown and crisp.

BOORTSOG (FRIED DOUGH)

Boortsog is a traditional Mongolian snack deep-fried in oil. Mongolians like to use oil that comes from the fat of cooking meat so that the *boortsog* has the flavor and aroma of the meat, but any vegetable oil will do.

10 cups (2.5 L) flour

3—4 (750 ml—1 L) cups sugar

½ cup (125 ml) butter

3 cups (750 ml) water

Salt to taste

Warm water

Oil for frying

- Mix sugar, salt, and butter in the warm water until dissolved. Slowly mix in flour. Turn the dough out onto a floured board and knead the mixture into a smooth, soft dough. It is important to work out all the air.
- Let the dough rest for a minute, then repeat kneading until all the air has been removed.
- Roll the dough out into a sheet ⅓—½ inch (1—1.5 cm) thick. Cut the dough into shapes. Traditionally, 1- to 1.5-inch (3—4 cm) wide strips are cut into rectangles and triangles, but cookie cutters can provide amusing alternatives. Now make two small and shallow cut lines to each piece to let out any remaining air and to add some decoration.
- Preheat the oil in a high-sided pot. Place in as many pieces of dough as the pot can handle without crowding, and fry them until golden brown. Remove the fried pieces with a metal strainer and place on a paper towel to soak up the excess oil. Continue until all the pieces have been fried.
- *Boortsog* is great with butter, jam, or cheese and can be stored for around a month. It is a favorite for snacking.

A B C D

1
2
3
4

RUSSIA

Hövsgöl

Uvs

Hyargas

Selenge
Darhan ●
Erdenet ●

Yöröö
Shatin

Hüyten
(Nayramadlin)
15,272 ft / 4,653 m)

Har Us

Dorgon

Hangai Range

Orhon

Ulaanbaatar ●

Hentii Range

Onon

Altai Range

Orkhon
Valley

Karakorum ●

Tuul

Herlen

Burkhan
Khalduun ▲

Xinjiang
Uighur
Autonomous
Region

G o b i

D e s e r t

PEOPLE'S REPUBLIC OF CHINA

● Capital city
● Major town
▲ Mountain peak

Feet		Meters
16,500		5,000
9,900		3,000
6,600		2,000
3,300		1,000
1,650		500
660		200
0		0

MAP OF MONGOLIA

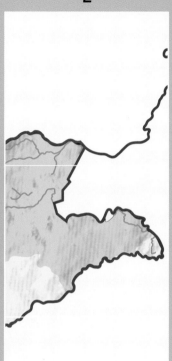

E

N

Altai Range, A2

Burkhan Khalduun
Mountain, D2

Darhan, C1

Erdenet, C2

Gobi Desert, B3,
C3, D3

Hangai Mountain
Range, B2
Hentii Mountain
Range, D2
Herlen River, D2
Hüyten Mountain,
A2

Karakorum, C2

Lake Dorgon, A2,
B2
Lake Har Us, A2
Lake Hövsgöl, B1,
C1
Lake Hyargas,
A1—A2
Lake Uvs, A1

Onon River, D1—D2
Orhon River, C2
Orkhon Valley, B2

People's Republic of
China, B3—B4,
C3—C4, D3—D4,
E1—E4

Russia, A1, B1, C1,
D1, E1

Selenge River, C1
Sharin River,
C1—C2

Tuul River, C2

Ulaanbaatar, C2,
D2

Xinjiang Uighur
Autonomous
Region, A2—A4

Yöröö River, C1, D1

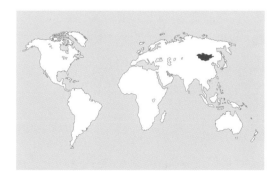

ECONOMIC MONGOLIA

Natural Resources

 Coal

 Copper

 Fluorine

 Gold

 Phosphorus

 Salt

 Timber

 Tin

Services

 Airport

 Tourism

Agriculture

 Camels

 Livestock

Manufacturing

 Textiles

ABOUT THE ECONOMY

OVERVIEW

Mongolia's economy has taken many dramatic swings since the demise of communism in 1990. The termination of Soviet financial assistance saw the gross domestic product (GDP) drop by a third almost overnight—and then the switch to a freer market economy set in motion rapid and dramatic growth. Being based largely on two industries, agriculture and mining, the Mongolian economy is highly susceptible to natural disaster and global commodity demands. Severe winter storms and relentless summer droughts from 2000 to 2002 put the GDP into negative numbers as livestock herds were decimated. Growth in world metals markets from 2004 to 2008 resulted in a rapid growth in the GDP of 9 percent per year and also sparked inflation to jump to nearly 40 percent. Then, in the face of the global financial tumult of 2008 to 2009, the economy declined again. Overall, Mongolia's economy is moving toward increased stability and prosperity as policies are modernized and the nation expands its international trade presence, though its reliance on only a few industries continues to be risky.

CURRENCY

Mongolian tögrög/tugrik (MNT)
1 tögrög/tugrik (MNT) = 100 möngö
US$1 = 1,449 MNT (August 2009)

GROSS DOMESTIC PRODUCT (GDP)

$9.56 billion (2008 estimate)

GDP PER CAPITA

$3,200 (2008 estimate)

LABOR FORCE

1.07 million (2008 estimate)

LABOR FORCE BY TYPE OF JOB

Agriculture: 34 percent
Industry: 5 percent
Services: 61 percent (2008 estimate)

UNEMPLOYMENT RATE

2.8 percent (2008 estimate)

INFLATION RATE

28 percent (2008 estimate)

MAIN INDUSTRIES

Agriculture; mining (coal, copper, molybdenum, fluorspar, tin, tungsten, and gold); construction and construction materials; oil; food and beverages; processing of animal products, cashmere and natural fiber manufacturing

MAIN EXPORTS

Copper, apparel, livestock, animal products, cashmere, wool, hides, fluorspar, other nonferrous metals, coal

MAIN IMPORTS

Machinery and equipment, fuel, cars, food products, industrial consumer goods, chemicals, building materials, sugar, tea

CULTURAL MONGOLIA

Uvs Nuur Basin
Made a world heritage site in 2003, the basin, which is shared with Russia, contains a large, shallow, and highly saline lake. The site is made up of a dozen protected areas and supports a wide range of birds and other animals, including the endangered snow leopard and a number of rare species of gerbil, jerboas, and the marbled polecat.

Amarbayasgalant Khiid Monastery
Situated in Selenge *aimag*, it is one of the three most important Buddhist monasteries in Mongolia. Originally built between 1726 and 1736 by the Manchu emperor Yongzheng, the monastery contains the mummified body of the sculptor and painter Zanabazar.

Gandan Monastery
Located in Ulaanbaatar, Gandan is the only monastery to survive the communist purges of the 1930s and '40s. Also called Gandantegchinlen, it is the biggest and most important monastery in all of Mongolia. It has been the main center of Buddhist learning in Mongolia since it was established in 1835. Though closed by the communists in 1938, Gandan was allowed to reopen in 1944 and operate under a minimal staff.

Museum of Natural History
Also located in Ulaanbaataar, the museum exhibits large collections of anthropological artifacts and important specimens in the areas of geology, zoology, botany, and paleontology. The museum was founded in 1966 and contains a significant number of dinosaur fossils from the region.

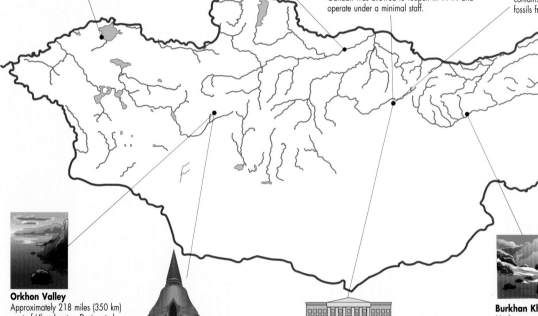

Orkhon Valley
Approximately 218 miles (350 km) west of Ulaanbaatar. Designated a UNESCO world heritage site in 2004, it is the locale of a number of historical places that document the development of nomadic pastoral traditions in the area over a span of more than 2,000 years. It was at the heart of the Mongolian Empire.

Erdene Zuu Monastery
Built in 1585, it is thought to be the oldest Buddhist monastery in Mongolia. It was damaged by warfare in the 1680s, rebuilt in the mid-18th century, and then mostly destroyed in the antireligious communist purges of 1939. Only three small temples and the external wall were left standing. It has now been restored to being an active monastery as well as a museum open to the public. Erdene Zuu is a part of the Orkhon Valley.

National Museum of Mongolian History
Located in the capital city of Ulaanbaatar, the National Museum is one of the main museums in Mongolia. Established in 1991 at the site of the old Museum of the Revolution, the museum is dedicated to preserving Mongolian culture and is involved in scientific and educational pursuits in the areas of historical, archaeological, and ethnographic studies.

Burkhan Khalduun Mountain
Made a protected area in 1992, the mountain was originally designated as sacred by Genghis Khan and is considered to be the most sacred mountain in Mongolia. It is part of the Khentii Mountains and is located in Khentii *aimag*. It is also widely believed to be both the birthplace and the site of the tomb of Genghis Khan.

ABOUT THE CULTURE

OFFICIAL NAME
Mongolia

LAND AREA
603,900 square miles (1,564,101 sq km)

CAPITAL
Ulaanbaatar

MAJOR CITIES
Ulaanbaatar, Èrdènèt, Darchan, Đojbalsan, Mörön

PROVINCES (*AIMAGS* OR *AYMAGS*)
1 municipality (Ulaanbaatar) plus 21 *aimags*: Arhangay, Bayanhongor, Bayan-Olgiy, Bulgan, Darchan-Uul, Dornod, Dornogovi, Dundgovi, Dzavhan (Zavkhan), Govi-Altay, Govisumber, Hentiy, Hovd, Hovsgol, Omnogovi, Orhon, Ovorhangay, Selenge, Suhbaatar, Tov, Uvs

MAJOR RIVERS
Emajõgi, Pärnu, Narva

HIGHEST POINT
Nayramadlin Orgil (Huyten Orgil) (14,350 feet/4,374 m)

MAJOR WATERWAYS
Lake Hovsgol, Lake Uvs, Lake Hövsgöl, Lake Har Us, Selenge River, Orhon River, Herlen River

POPULATION
3,041,142 (2009 estimate)

LIFE EXPECTANCY
Total population: 67.65 years
Male: 65.23 years
Female: 70.19 years (2008 estimate)

BIRTHRATE
2.23 children born per female (2009 estimate)

ETHNIC GROUPS
Mongol (mostly Khalkha) 94.9 percent, Turkic (mostly Kazakh) 5 percent, other (including Chinese and Russian) 0.1 percent (2000 estimate)

LITERACY RATE
97.8 percent of the population over 15 can read and write.
Male: 98 percent; female: 97.5 percent (2000 census)

RELIGION
Buddhist Lamaist 50 percent, Shamanist and Christian 6 percent, Muslim 4 percent, none 40 percent (2004 estimate)

LANGUAGES
Khalkha Mongol 90 percent, Turkic and Russian 10 percent (1999 estimate)

TIME LINE

IN MONGOLIA	IN THE WORLD
3rd century B.C. Xiongnu invasion of China fails. **2nd–1st centuries** B.C. Nomadic peoples move farther west near China. **317** A.D. Xianbei conquer northern China. **1196–1206** Temüjin unifies the Mongols and assumes the title of Genghis (Chinggis) Khan. **1206–15** Genghis expands the Mongolian Empire south to Beijing and west to Lake Balkash. **1220–26** Most of southwest Asia conquered. Invasion of Europe and China. **1227** Genghis dies during the siege of Hsingchungfu. Son Ogedei becomes Khan. **1231** Invasion of Korean Peninsula. **1235** Capital rebuilt at Karakorum. **1237–41** Invasion of Europe. Ends at Vienna with the death of Ogedei. **1261** Kublai is made Great Khan. **1391** Timur defeats the Golden Horde. **1400–54** Empire crumbles under civil war. **1586** Buddhism becomes the main religion. **1636** Inner Mongolia created. **1691** Outer Mongolia created. **1911** Qing dynasty falls. Outer Mongolia becomes independent. **1919** Occupation by Chinese army. **1920** Mongolian People's Party formed.	**116–17** B.C. The Roman Empire reach its greatest extent, under Emperor Trajan (98–17). **1206–1368** Genghis Khan unifies the Mongols and starts conquest of the world. At its height, the Mongol Empire under Kublai Khan stretches from China to Persia and parts of Europe and Russia. **1530** Beginning of transatlantic slave trade organized by the Portuguese in Africa. **1789–99** The French Revolution **1914** World War I begins.

IN MONGOLIA	IN THE WORLD

1921
Mongolian "People's Government" formed.

1924
Mongolian People's Revolutionary Party (MPRP) formed, birth of the Mongolian People's Republic.

1939
World War II begins.

1945
Mongolians vote for independence in a UN plebiscite.

1945
The United States drops atomic bombs on Hiroshima and Nagasaki. World War II ends.

1952
Prime Minister Horloogiyn Choybalsan dies, and is replaced by Yu Tsedenbal.

1955–60
Mongolian herds successfully collectivized.

1965
Tsedenbal purges the intelligentsia.

1966
The Chinese Cultural Revolution.

1984
Tsedenbal resigns.
Mongolian Democratic Association formed.

1986
Nuclear power disaster at Chernobyl in Ukraine.

1990
First democratic elections are held. The MPRP wins. The first elected People's Great Hural takes office.

1991
Breakup of the Soviet Union.

1993
First direct presidential election is held and won by the opposition candidate Punsalmaagiyn Ochirbat.

1996
Opposition wins elections and forms first noncommunist government.

1997
Hong Kong is returned to China.

2000
MPRP wins elections, Nambaryn Enkhbayar becomes prime minister.

2001
Terrorists crash planes into New York, Washington D.C., and Pennsylvania.

2004
Election is split. MPRP forms coalition government headed by Tsakhia Elbegdorj.

2006
Coalition government dissolved by MPRP, new coalition formed by Miyeegombyn Enkhbold.

2007
Enkhbold's coalition dissolves; new coalition formed under Sanjaagiin Bayar.

2008
MPRP forms new government, again under Bayar.

GLOSSARY

aimag or **aymag** (AI-mug)
A province or political subdivision, like states, of which there are 21 in Mongolia.

airag (AI-rug)
Fermented mare's milk.

arkhi (AHR-khee)
Alcoholic drink distilled from cow's milk.

Bielgee (BEE-el-gee)
Mongolian dance performed solo by a girl.

buuz (BUHZ)
Fried dumpling; a pastry filled with ground lamb.

del (DEHL)
Mongolian traditional outer garment worn by both men and women.

ger (GUHR) or **yurt**
Portable tent dwelling made of felt.

Khalkha (HAL-ha)
Means shield or alliance. A nomadic people living in eastern and central Mongolia.

khoomi (KHAW-me)
Throat singing.

lama
Buddhist monk.

morin khuur (MAW-rin kher)
Two-stringed Mongolian fiddle with a head shaped like a horse's head.

örtöö (OOR-taw)
Relay station for the courier system of horse riders.

ovoo (AW-waw)
Mound of rocks to honor various gods and spirits; a rustic shrine.

shudrag (SHOOD-rug)
Three-stringed Mongolian lute.

Silk Road
An ancient trade route linking China and imperial Rome, named for the silk transported on it. Caravans generally met on the road and traded goods and news.

Soyombo (SOH-yom-bo)
Mongolian symbol on the national flag consisting of a flame, a sun, a crescent moon, two intertwined fish (yin-yang), rectangles, and triangles.

State Great Hural
The Mongolian one-house parliament.

Tengri (TENG-ri)
The Supreme or Eternal Sky God.

tögrög (TOOG-roog)
Mongolian currency.

yoching (YAW-ching)
Mongolian zither with metal pieces stretched on a board, played by striking with two hammers.

zurag (ZOO-rug)
A two-dimensional painting style in Mongolia that uses distinctive colors and depicts the traditional lifestyle.

FOR FURTHER INFORMATION

BOOKS

Hanson, Jennifer L. *Mongolia* (Nations in Transition). New York: Facts on File, 2003.

Lassieur, Allison. *Mongolia* (Enchantment of the World). New York: Children's Press, 2007.

Lewin, Ted and Betsy Lewin. *Horse Song: The Nadaam of Mongolia*. New York: Lee and Low Books, 2008.

Morgan, David. *The Mongols*. Malden, MA: Blackwell Publishers, 2007.

Reynolds, Jan. *Mongolia* (Vanishing Cultures). New York: Lee and Low Books, 2007.

Waugh, Louise. *Hearing Birds Fly: A Nomadic Year in Mongolia.* London: Little, Brown Book Group, 2003.

FILMS

Byambasuren Davaa. *Cave of the Yellow Dog*. Tartan Video, 2007.

Luigi Falorni and Byambasuren Davaa. *The Story of the Weeping Camel.* New Line Home Video, 2005.

MUSIC

Various artists. *Folk Music of Mongolia; The Land of Genghis Khan.* Collectable Records, 2007.

Various artists. *Mongolia—Living Music of the Steppes.* Music of the Earth, 2009.

BIBLIOGRAPHY

BOOKS

Avery, Martha. *Women of Mongolia.* Boulder, CO: Asian Art & Archaeology, 1996.

Brill, Marlene Targ. *Mongolia* (Enchantment of the World). Chicago: Children's Press, 1992.

Goldstein, Melvyn C. and Cynthia M. Beall. *The Changing World of Mongolia's Nomads.* Los Angeles: University of California Press, 1994.

Major, John S. *The Land and People of Mongolia.* New York: J. B. Lippincott, 1990.

Middleton, Nick. *The Last Disco in Outer Mongolia.* London: Sinclair-Stevenson Ltd, 1992.

Severin, Tim. *In Search of Genghis Khan: An Exhilarating Journey on Horseback across the Steppes of Mongolia.* New York: Cooper Square Press, 2003.

WEBSITES

British Broadcasting Corporation: Timeline: Mongolia. http://news.bbc.co.uk/2/hi/asia-pacific/1235612.stm

CIA: The World Factbook (Select Mongolia). www.cia.gov/library/publications/the-world-factbook/

Climate Mongolia: Average Temperatures and Rainfall. www.studentsoftheworld.info/pageinfo_pays.php3?Pays=MNG&Opt=climate

Earth Trends: Biodiversity and Protected Areas—Mongolia. http://earthtrends.wri.org/pdf_library/country_profiles/bio_cou_496.pdf

Embassy of Mongolia, Washington, DC: Economy and Trade. www.mongolianembassy.us/eng_economy_and_trade/economy_and_trade.php

ERINA (Economic Research Institute for Northeast Asia): The Mongolian Livestock Sector. www.erina.or.jp/en/Research/db/pdf2002/02160e.pdf

Foreign Investment and Foreign Trade Agency: Mongolia. www.investmongolia.com/index.php?sel=menu&mnl=5_8

Mongolia Timeline. http://ancienthistory.about.com/od/timelines/a/Mongoliatime.htm

National Parks of Mongolia. www.nationalparks-worldwide.info/mongolia.htm

Official Tourism Website of Mongolia. www.mongoliatourism.gov.mn.

United Nations Environment Programme: Mongolia: State of the Environment—Land Degradation. www.rrcap.unep.org/pub/soe/mongolia_land.pdf

United States Department of State: Background Note: Mongolia. www.state.gov/r/pa/ei/bgn/2779.htm

World Bank, The. East Asia Update—Mongolia Overview. http://web.worldbank.org/WBSITE/EXTERNAL/COUNTRIES/EASTASIAPACIFICEXT/EXTEAPHALFYEARLYUPDATE/0,,contentMDK:20708484~isCURL:Y~menuPK:550232~pagePK:64168445~piPK:64168309~theSitePK:550226,00.html

World Facts Index: Facts about Mongolia: http://worldfacts.us/Mongolia.htmi

INDEX

INDEX